GET MORE DATES
THAN YOUR SKINNY FRIENDS

A Curvy Girl's Guide
to Conquering Men and the Competition

GET MORE DATES
THAN YOUR SKINNY FRIENDS

*A Curvy Girl's Guide
to Conquering Men and the Competition*

Kat Bacon

LANGDON STREET PRESS, MINNEAPOLIS MN

Langdon Street Press
212 3rd Avenue North, Suite 290
Minneapolis, MN 55401
612.455.2293
www.langdonstreetpress.com

ISBN-13: 978-1-62652-165-0
LCCN: 2013939500

Distributed by Itasca Books

Edited by Spencer Curry
Cover Design by Gwendy Gayle Hollanes
Typeset by James Arneson
Author Photo by Penny Silvia Photography

Printed in the United States of America

05/14

3 0966 00132 4421

This book is dedicated to the love of my life, Scott, and my son, Spencer. Your unconditional love and encouragement motivates me to be my best every day. I love and cherish you both.

Contents

Acknowledgments   ix

Introduction   1

Part 1

Becoming a Confident Curvy Girl (CCG) ~ *Getting Ready, Inside and Out, for Some Amazing Dates*

Chapter One   Confident Curvy Girl 101   7

Chapter Two   Lights, Camera, Life!   29

Chapter Three The Male Mystique   45

Chapter Four   Ditch the "Rules" and Get SASSY   55

Chapter Five   Be Buzz-Worthy   57

Chapter Six   Brand Yourself   61

Chapter Seven Work It Out   73

Chapter Eight Clean Up Your Act, Your Story's Getting Dusty   81

Part 2

Unleash Your Curve Appeal ~ *Finding Incredible Dates*

Chapter Nine   It's Not All About You   87

Chapter Ten   Throw Away Your List   91

Chapter Eleven Don't Let That Skinny Chick Take Your Guy   97

Chapter Twelve   Ready, Aim, Fire!   107

Chapter Thirteen   Online Optimization   117

Part 3
It's Raining Men ~ *First Date and Beyond*

Chapter Fourteen   The "Where Have You Been All
                      My Life?" First Date   131

Chapter Fifteen   The Jury's In   137

Chapter Sixteen   Textually Active   143

Chapter Seventeen   It's Your Time   147

Chapter Eighteen   FAQ—Your Dating Questions Answered 149

Afterword   153
Sources   159
About the Author   160

Acknowledgments

Thank you, dear curvy girl, for believing in yourself enough to purchase this book. It was written with your struggles in mind and will teach you, step-by-step, how to be hot, healthy, and happy while turning the head of any guy.

Thank you to my friends and family who supported me through this endeavor, offering their advice and critical eyes. I couldn't have done it without the help of Dana, Michelle, Catherine, Sukhi, Kimberly, Linda, Scott, and my mother, Susan.

I offer my heartfelt gratitude to my father, Gary, who always taught me to believe in myself and to set my goals high.

A special thank-you to my son, Spencer, for being my fabulous editor and for providing his ideas and thoughts throughout the entire book-writing process.

Introduction

*D*o you walk into a room and scan the women to see who is skinnier than you? If so, this book is for you.

I'm going to teach you how to be hot, healthy, and happy in that wonderful curvy body of yours. In short, I'm going to show you how to be a CCG.

What is a CCG? It's an acronym for Confident Curvy Girl, and it's also the essence of everything you will learn in the following pages. Being confident is the key to attracting dates—yes, even *more* dates than your skinny friends.

By the time you finish reading this book, you'll still scan the room. But you'll be looking for potential dates, not skinny competitors. You will be so confident in your own skin that other girls won't matter to you. In fact, the skinny girls will be jealous of *you* because you'll radiate a positive energy that will attract men while leaving other women in the dust.

This book is the product of nearly three decades of dating experience and features the collective wisdom and life experiences of dozens of curvy girls. You will share in their successes and failures, their triumphs and follies. In learning from others' experiences, we greatly improve our own odds of success. After all, those who study history are less likely to repeat it.

Just as every curvy girl is unique, so too is this book.

Throughout my twenties, thirties, and now forties, I noticed a painful shortage of books that directly address the specific challenges of dating as an overweight woman—or, as I will refer to it in this book, curvy.

I was born curvy—or, as my parents labeled it, "big boned." In third grade, I was doing aerobics with the teachers at my elementary school. I was on Weight Watchers by age twelve.

Despite my weight problem, I was very active. PE was my favorite subject in school, and I loved organized team sports like softball and soccer. I rode my bike everywhere, played tennis, and swam every chance I had during the summer. Mom always packed healthy foods in my lunch box and only allowed my sister and me zero-calorie drinks.

Since then, I have been on every diet imaginable—twice. I've tried Nutrisystem, Jenny Craig, the OPTIFAST liquid diet, Isagenix cleanses, the Hollywood Diet, South Beach, Atkins, the maple syrup and cayenne pepper diets, the Sunrider Tea diet, good ol' calorie counting, and many others.

I've also had Lap-Band surgery, a medical procedure that creates a smaller stomach pouch and severely restricts the kinds of food I can eat. Despite the fact that I can only consume half of what I used to, I'm still curvy!

I'm now being told by dieticians that I'm curvy because I don't eat *enough*. I have also been told if I'm hardly eating, it must be my thyroid—except that it's been tested six times and is fine. A sugar allergy became the next possible culprit, so I went through acupuncture allergy cleansing. It fixed my allergies to grasses but not my fat.

Hormones? Nope. Okay, it must be because I have a leaky gut
—yes, that is what one doctor told me. I went on the "leaky-gut
diet," and sure enough, I'm still curvy.

The bottom line is, I'm *curvy*. Yes, curvy! God made me this
way, and I just need to love and accept myself the way I am. It
isn't always easy, but I'm fighting the good fight—and winning!
By reading this book, you will learn how to triumphantly win
your own battle too.

Along with being born with "big bones," I was also born with
a love of boys—hardly an ideal combination. When I was still in
diapers, I crawled next door to be with the little neighbor boy.
Through grade school, I had countless crushes and "boyfriends";
to this day, I can still recall their names and what it was about
them that made me swoon.

Yes, I was boy crazy, and I still am.

My love for men overrode my body-image issues and made
learning the art of attraction a necessity. I have learned this skill
over a span of almost forty years. The number of men I've dated
cracks triple digits. I've had incredible romances, many long-term
relationships, and four marriage proposals, not including three
other suitors that said they would propose if I promised to say yes.

I know what you're thinking: anybody can catch a certified
goober or man-child living with his mom. Let me assure you
that most of the guys I dated were good-looking. My high school
sweetheart won "best body" during his senior year and was referred
to as "godlike" by more than a few frenemies at school. My first
husband was widely considered handsome. I've also dated highly
successful men, from CEOs to tech executives.

Granted, they weren't *all* handsome and successful, but I want
to make the point that my dating strategies attract all kinds of
men—even the ones your skinny friends would kill for.

Fortunately, I was born into a family that prizes positive thinking and inspiration. As a young girl, my father made me listen to Zig Ziglar, an oddly named but unnervingly skilled motivational speaker. I had to say positive affirmations every day and read books like *The Magic of Believing*. I'm still a positive-thinking junkie; I spend a lot of my time reading and listening to the inspirational messages of Wayne Dyer, Joel Osteen, Tony Robbins, and Leo Buscaglia.

As a female executive in a male-dominated industry, my career has provided me with access to the boys' clubhouse, so to speak. Over the past twenty years, I have learned what motivates men and which girls turn their heads.

You may be thinking: what's the catch? Here's the thing: there isn't one.

You needn't be fabulously wealthy, stunningly beautiful, or Mensa smart to make this book work for you.

Like all women, I have my own flaws. My weight fluctuates on a daily basis. Picking something from my closet that fits is like a constant game of Russian roulette. I have large legs, I still get acne, and I have stretch marks on my stomach—not to mention the scars caused by my Lap-Band surgery. My cooking skills are limited to pouring milk on cereal and assembling sandwiches. I suffer from mild social anxiety and, on top of it all, I was a single mother at age twenty. Hardly a recipe for a man-eater.

Even with those strikes against me, I never wanted for dates. I am living proof that dating success has more to do with behavior than physical attributes or an attractive skill set.

Though this book is focused on dating, I hope the principles you learn will prove useful in other aspects of your life. I believe with all of my heart that this book will transform you from a "fat girl" to a Confident Curvy Girl.

Part 1

Becoming a Confident Curvy Girl (CCG)

Getting Ready, Inside and Out, for Some Amazing Dates

"Don't worry about finding the right guy
—concentrate on becoming the right girl."
~Kat Bacon

Chapter One

Confident Curvy Girl 101

"Self-esteem isn't everything; it's just that there's nothing without it."
~Gloria Steinem

While a healthy level of self-esteem can be all too rare in today's world, the problem is even more pronounced in curvy girls.

Modern society bombards curvy women with pictures of size-0 models, actresses who look like they're waiting for a UN food drop, and female sports figures with bodies honed to perfection through years of torturous training.

Much like TV shows that portray affluent families as average, even so-called "reality stars" bear little resemblance to reality. There is nothing average about the women from the *Real House-wives* franchise or whatever Kardashian spin-off is currently airing.

When popular magazines lambast a size-6 celebrity as "chunky," what message is society sending curvy girls?

The truth is that the emphasis on stick-thin figures is female-driven. While a man might assess a woman's attractiveness or sense of humor, her fellow females will focus on her size or choice of clothes. Women prefer tightly identified categories (style of hair, color of nails, or brand of handbag, for example) that are judged by way of comparison with themselves. In contrast, guys' areas of interest are broad, with many definitions of good; there's always more than one way to be appealing.

You've probably known an average or even unattractive girl who had men swooning. I've known several of these girls in my life. I scratch my head and think, "She must possess some top-shelf pheromones." I went to high school with one of these girls. She was average in most respects, including looks, intelligence, and popularity. But she had one quality that wasn't average: her self-esteem. While other girls were mostly indifferent to Amanda—she was neither envied nor pitied—our male counterparts were not so unmoved. They fell over themselves for the opportunity to date her.

So what did Amanda have going for her? Well, for one, she thought her shit didn't stink! She didn't accept the consensus of her female peers that she was nothing to write home about; she thought she was the bomb, and the boys bought it. Amanda was confident, confident, confident.

Coincidentally, a close friend's husband went to college with Amanda and testified that none of her black magic had worn off. All of his friends lined up to date her. Even into adulthood, Amanda had the pick of any man she wanted.

Think back to "your" Amanda. I bet she exuded confidence and had a sex appeal that came from the inside.

This inner confidence and admiration doesn't just work for skinny women. It also works for curvy girls. If you love and have confidence in yourself, the guys will follow your lead.

WHY MEN LIKE BITCHY WOMEN

You may be thinking, "What about the bitchy, awful, high-maintenance girls? Why do they seem to attract all of the guys?" It's simple. Bitchy women get the guys because they make men believe that they are superior women and therefore men are lucky to be with them. They walk into every room acting like they're the hottest thing since sliced bread, exuding attitude and an easy confidence.

My girlfriend Catherine is confidence personified. She is a curvy girl with the attitude of a supermodel. Catherine is a perfect example of how it doesn't matter how much you weigh. What counts is how you perceive yourself.

A few years ago, while vacationing in Maui, I met a hot cabana boy. After I found out he was from a town neighboring mine in Northern California, we became friendly with each other. He was twenty-three years old and adorable.

Although I was single, there was not one minute that I thought that he could ever be attracted to me. I'm not exactly at the top of my game in my preferred resort wear: no makeup, hair in a ponytail, and wearing the least curve-friendly article of clothing: a swimsuit. In that setting, attracting a guy is the last thing on my mind.

The next year, I took Catherine with me to Maui, and we stayed at the same hotel. My traveling companion was curvy, single, and fifty-two years old when I introduced her to my friend, the cabana boy. From the moment she laid eyes on him, the flirting started. I rolled my eyes and laughed at the notion that she could bag a man less than half her age. But sure enough, within forty-eight hours, she and the cabana boy were an item. They saw each other several times during our weeklong stay.

It was *all* in her attitude. Catherine believed she could get a hot twenty-four-year-old, and she did!

If I thought the hookup was a fluke, I was proven wrong when she returned home and started dating a handsome, fit, attractive—and yes, *younger*—winery owner. They dated for a year and a half before she broke his heart.

Catherine gets nothing but the best because she won't settle for less. She has taught me more about the power of confidence than anyone I know. She sets high standards for herself and expects the men she's with to meet them. I always believed that confidence came with skinniness, but Catherine proved that confidence comes in *all* sizes!

Your past dating experiences may have discouraged you from getting back into the game. You might envy your skinny friends and the ease with which they seem to get dates.

But like Catherine, if you learn to believe in yourself, you will get more dates than your skinny friends. If you are diligent in bettering yourself and *confident* that you've got great things coming, your skinny friends will become envious of *you*.

Confidence is not a switch you turn on overnight. You are not going to be totally confident 100 percent of the time. Don't be too hard on yourself if you don't master it right away. It is natural to have moments of nervousness, fear, and insecurity. Confidence is a learnable skill that requires constant practice.

A professional basketball player may be able to make forty-nine baskets in a row but still miss the fiftieth. In truth, practice makes *better* but never perfect.

The best way to be confident is to simply learn to take the right action.

Learn my seven confidence-building steps and put them into practice. You will find that your confidence grows naturally.

CCG STEP #1
Be Your Greatest Love

"Love yourself first and everything falls into line."
~Lucille Ball

The inability to love one's self has been the downfall of many curvy girls.

Marilyn Monroe was one of the biggest stars of the twentieth century, yet she never possessed enough confidence to love herself on her own terms. She was adored by millions but not by the most important person of all: herself.

It's a vicious cycle: people who don't love themselves often invite negative reinforcement, which only serves to cement their poor self image.

Learning to appreciate yourself is an essential component of confidence. If you don't love yourself, why would anyone else?

When you say mean things to yourself ("I'm fat, I'm ugly, I'm unattractive"), you merely reinforce your negative self-view.

Change your energy and increase your magnetism by simply affirming that you love yourself. Take a page from motivational speaker Brian Tracy, who suggests that you repeat "I like myself" fifty times a day. While that might seem excessive, the principle is a sound one; reinforcement of positivity is a habit every CCG must have. It will feel uncomfortable at first, but after you are done getting ready in the morning, look at yourself in the mirror and give yourself one compliment. Try "You look wonderful,"

"You look hot," "You have a great smile," "Your hair looks amazing," or "I love every inch of you." And don't forget to say "I like myself."

A firm belief in yourself will attract positive things to your life. As Derek Gamba said, "You cannot make someone love you. You can only make yourself someone who can be loved."

A few years ago I was complaining about the fact that my boobs were not as perky as they once were. I thought about the possibility of getting breast implants. My brother-in-law said, "Why would you do that? Guys like *all* boobs. Small, medium, big, perky, droopy—whatever. They like them all."

I was confused and said, "Don't you like all boobs to look like the pictures in *Playboy*?"

"No way," he replied. "There has never been a boob I didn't like."

All this time, I had believed that men universally preferred this feminine "ideal," but really I was the one with the "perfect picture." We must concentrate on loving ourselves exactly the way we are.

Curvy Contemplation

Write down three positive affirmations you can say to yourself each morning.

1.
2.
3.

And don't forget to say "I like myself."

"You yourself, as much as anybody in the entire universe, deserve your love and affection."

~Buddha

CCG STEP #2
Get Your Curve On

To me, beauty is about being comfortable in your own skin. It's about knowing and accepting who you are."

~Ellen DeGeneres

We live in a society where most women hate their appearance. Why is this?

Because billions of dollars are spent every year on advertising to make you feel like you aren't good enough the way you are. We see messages every day that tell us we need to plump up our lips, whiten our teeth, tan our skin, suck out our fat, rub out our cellulite, de-wrinkle our skin. . . . The list of self-improvements is endless.

The more we believe these messages, the more products and services we buy to fix our so-called flaws.

I Get You!

Whether you are ten pounds or 200 pounds overweight, you judge yourself based on what your scale says. Your self-worth comes from that number, and you still hold on to a dream that you will be skinny someday. You wholeheartedly believe that everything in life—especially your dating life—will be perfect as soon as you can just drop those extra pounds.

If this is you, guess what? You don't have to identify with those negative feelings anymore. If you are active, healthy, and happy, you don't need to change your curviness in order to be "adequate." Do not fall into the media trap of thinking that you need fixing.

According to a recent study, 63.7 percent of all women in the USA are overweight or obese;[1] the average size of the American female now stands at 14.[2] Globally, 30 percent of all women are classified as overweight or obese.[3]

In short, quit beating yourself up!

SIGNS YOU MAY BE IN NEED OF A CCG INTERVENTION

1. You have fantasies that start with "If I start dieting now, I will be skinny by [insert event]." I tend to do this every time I have a trip planned, a high school reunion to attend, or any other special event at which I know I'll want to impress people.

2. The thought of losing weight is always on your mind. It creeps in and out of your thoughts all day long. In fact, most decisions you make—or don't make—are influenced by your weight.

3. You pass up fun opportunities because you don't feel like you look good in the appropriate attire: a bathing suit, tennis skirt, sleeveless dress, wet suit, shorts, costume, or party dress.

4. You dread being a bridesmaid because you are afraid the bride is going to put you in an unflattering dress or that the skinny bridesmaids will make you look big. You pray that you'll be able to wear something that covers your problem areas—arms, tummy, and legs.

5. You say no to parties, events, or even dates because you feel like you look too fat.

6. You turn down fun nights out at the club because you assume none of the guys will like you and you will come home disappointed.
7. The thought of your guy seeing you naked for the first time is terrifying. You think to yourself, "I sure hope he doesn't want to get it on in the broad daylight!" The mere thought fills you with anxiety.
8. You want to work out at the gym, but you feel uncomfortable doing the downward dog yoga pose or jiggling on the treadmill in front of all the gym rats.
9. You are convinced that you are undisciplined, unmotivated, unattractive, undesirable, and undeserving. You believe that you have no self-control or willpower, because if you did, you would be skinny like everyone else.
10. It just feels more comfortable not to put yourself out there because of the fear of rejection.

I believe there are two types of curvy girls.

Type I Curvy Girl

Type I curvy girls were born curvy and have struggled with their weight most of their lives. They've tried countless diets only to gain back more weight than they lost. Often, they eat the same as (or less than) their friends but are still curvier.

If this describes you, then your weight has little to do with your willpower, discipline, or activity level and everything to do with your physiology. Let me say this in a different way: your full figure is not your fault! This may go against everything that you've been told all of your life, but it's true.

Look at Oprah Winfrey: she is one of the most famous women in the world and has every resource at her fingertips—and she is still curvy. She can hire the best chefs in the world to cook low-calorie, healthy meals, but she is still curvy. Other celebrities who struggle with their weight despite enviable resources include Carnie Wilson and Kirstie Alley.

To feel happier, more confident, and ready to take on every adventure, you don't need to change your weight. You need to change how you feel about yourself.

You may be thinking, "If I just accept myself, I'm giving up." But the opposite is actually true. By accepting yourself, you are taking charge of your life, your happiness, and your self-image. That doesn't give you permission to go crazy with your friends Ben and Jerry or to give up your exercise regimen. The point is to accept yourself exactly the way you are and to acknowledge and dismiss those self-defeating thoughts.

Weight gain is caused by consuming more calories than the body needs. Society wants you to believe this is caused by eating a diet high in fat and calories, living an inactive lifestyle, or both. However, studies show that the imbalance between calories consumed and calories burned may be caused by a number of different physiological factors, including genetic and hormonal conditions. In fact, there can be quite a few other major culprits.

It's in the genes. There is resounding evidence that heredity plays a major role in your weight. Studies of identical twins that have been raised apart have found that they weigh almost the same amount. Also, adopted children tend to have a weight similar to and resemble their biological parents more so than they do their adoptive parents. This demonstrates that body size is often more about nature and less about nurture. The fact is that your chances of being overweight are greater if one or both of your parents are overweight.

Health conditions. Hormonal challenges can cause a person to be overweight. Some common hormonal problems include underactive thyroid (hypothyroidism), Cushing's syndrome, and polycystic ovarian syndrome (PCOS).

Metabolism. Metabolic rates are often the result of heredity and are locked in at an early age. Studies have shown that children with overweight parents have slower metabolic rates. Also, a person's metabolism may slow as a result of chronic yo-yo dieting.

Fat cells. You can't diet away fat cells, and you can't work them off, either. Once you gain fat cells, they are there to stay.

Here's how it works. When you gain weight, your fat cells get bigger. When they can't grow any more, they multiply. When you try to lose weight, you don't lose the extra fat cells. You can shrink them to "normal" size, but in essence, you will never be as small as when you started.

So let's say you gain weight again. You have now created more fat cells that never go away and can at best be normal size. After years and years of yo-yo dieting, you could have billions and billions of extra fat cells. This could be why all of the chronic dieters you know are still overweight.

Type II Curvy Girl

The second type of curvy girl has recently become curvy due to pregnancy, stress eating, medication, quitting smoking, injury, menopause, addiction, or depression.

If this is you, you may be having a very difficult time accepting your new body.

The girl who is born heavy has had years to accept and maneuver around it. But girls who grew up thin and became curvy in later years often feel like they are a visitor in someone else's body. They frequently walk by a mirror and have to do a double take because they don't recognize themselves.

It's time to get real. If you've gone through menopause, are on medication that makes it impossible to lose weight, or have an injury that limits your physical activity, you most likely need to embrace your curviness—because it may be here for the long haul.

I realize I may have just dashed all of your hopes and dreams of how wonderful your life is going to be when you are thin again. But I want you to see the situation as it is. Nothing is impossible, but some situations are more challenging than others.

What you are going through is not your fault! You are not a lazy or bad person because you put on some pounds. Concentrate on accepting yourself exactly how you are today. Start by making it your goal to be the best, most amazing curvy girl you can be. Focus on applying the principles you will learn in this book, and if you do ever get back to your goal weight, you will be a double threat!

Curvy Contemplation

What type of curvy girl do you think you are? Type I or Type II? If you're Type II, are you a "guest" or a "resident" in our curvy society? Are you ready to accept yourself today, exactly the way you are?

_____

_____

_____

If you have just had a baby, quit smoking, or got out of a stressful situation, you may have joined the curvy culture for only a short time. If you have been thin most of your life, it is probable that you can get back into your skinny jeans again. But don't stop living and loving yourself *today*. You need to accept who you are right now, even if your plan is to get back to your normal size.

The reality is, if you don't accept yourself and your body type, the men who are looking for you don't have a chance.

CCG STEP #3
Don't Be a Phooey Vuitton

"Always be a first-rate version of yourself, instead of a second-rate version of somebody else."

~Judy Garland

A fake designer bag seems like a no-brainer: get the luxury look you want without the luxury price tag. Until the handle breaks. Or you see someone with the genuine article snickering at your knockoff.

A replica will never match up to the real thing because it's dishonest; whatever qualities made the original special are lost in translation.

While a fake handbag can be thrown out, a fake person isn't as easy to fix. Famous poet Friedrich Klopstock advised, "To only dream of the person you are supposed to be is to waste the person you are."

Curvy girls, please don't spend your life longing to be somebody else. You will only end up disappointed and sad.

I used to fantasize about being granted one wish. I wouldn't wish for world peace, good health, or riches. I would wish to be skinny. Not only to be skinny, but to be able to eat anything I wanted and still be skinny. I have moments of feeling this way even now, but I remind myself of my personal mantra: "I am hot, healthy, and happy. Everywhere I go, men are attracted to me." (We'll talk more about personal mantras later in the book.)

In order to attract men, you need to recognize just how truly magnificent you are!

"Most of our challenges in life come from not knowing ourselves and ignoring our true virtues."

~John Mason, American drama critic and author

The key to recognizing your awesomeness is to make a list of your attributes. Ideas for your list could include:

- Good friend
- Honest
- Hardworking
- Pretty hair
- Intelligent
- Caring
- Good cook
- Generous

After writing your list, ask your friends and family what they think your best attributes are. You will be surprised by all the magnificent qualities you have of which you weren't even aware. Read your list at least once a day and keep it in a place that you can get to easily when your confidence is weak.

"Be what you are. This is the first step toward becoming better than you are."

~Julius Hare, theological writer

Curvy Contemplation

Make a list of your good attributes. Try to write down at least eight.

1.
2.
3.
4.
5.
6.
7.
8.

CCG STEP #4

Fire Your Worst Critic

"Change the way you speak about yourself
and you can change your life."

~Joel Osteen, author and pastor

Many of us have put negative ideas into our subconscious that replay in our minds over and over again. Think about some of the negative "tapes" you may have going through your head. Some common themes are:

1. I'm not skinny enough.
2. I'll never find someone.
3. All men are shallow.

We also store up negative tapes from critical statements that others have made about us. Sometimes these tapes date all the way back to grade school—things like a mean remark made by a girl in your second-grade class, a rejection from a boy when you were fourteen, or a criticism that came from a well-meaning parent.

"My biggest problem is that I believe
almost everything I tell myself."
~Anonymous

These thoughts and prejudices hold us back from being fully alive, taking chances, and radiating confidence. Have you ever stopped to consider how different our lives would be if we only remembered the good things?

Change "Men don't like me because I'm fat" to "I know I look and feel good, and any man would be lucky to have me." Zig Ziglar wrote: "What you picture in your mind, your mind will go to work to accomplish." When addressing yourself, your litmus test should be: "Would my best friend call me fat or huge?" (If the answer is yes, you need a new bestie, stat.)

It is important to review the negative terms you use to describe yourself and to begin to use positive words instead. Instead of referring to yourself as overweight, fat, big, or huge, say you're curvy or voluptuous. This habit of thinking and saying negative things about yourself may be hard to break, but doing so will help you look at yourself in a more positive light over time.

Remember, a CCG always, always refers to herself as curvy, never fat.

"Our words set the direction for our lives."
~Joel Osteen

Curvy Contemplation

What negative tapes do you play repeatedly in your mind?

1.

2.

3.

What positive statements are you going to use to replace them?

1.

2.

3.

CCG STEP #5

Stop Comparing and Start Appreciating

"Why compare yourself with others? No one in the entire world can do a better job of being you than you."

~Anonymous

To be envious is to be human. Whether it's someone else's car, marriage, or body, a person possessing something you desire only serves to amplify your own perceived shortcomings.

What you don't know, however, is that the object of your envy may be two months behind on that Lexus payment. Her marriage might be on the rocks. Or maybe she can't even appreciate her own body due to low self-esteem. Trust me: "Miss Perfect" has problems too.

Habitually comparing yourself to others is a recipe for misery. It's easy to exaggerate attributes and qualities you don't like about yourself when compared against a perfect-but-incomplete picture.

When curvy girls constantly compare themselves to skinny girls, they can become bitter, jealous, and sad. There will always be girls who are skinnier than you. It's a waste of time and energy to compare yourself to other girls. Your life is too valuable to spend wanting what others have.

You are unique, endowed with qualities that are yours alone. You may think someone is better than you because she has skinnier legs or fuller lips, but that doesn't mean the guys who are attracted to you would agree.

My great-grandfather once saw a woman's large, "stovepipe" legs showing under a curtain and told his brother, "I'm going to marry her"—and he did! He liked big legs more than skinny legs, just like some other guys like flat-chested women while others like huge boobs.

Success in dating and in life is about being *your* best and not worrying about how someone else looks or what they are doing. You need to concentrate on rocking what *you* have, because you are the only one who has it!

CCG STEP #6
Learn the Magic of Mantras

"Self-worth comes from one thing
—thinking that you are worthy."
~*Wayne Dyer, self-help author and motivational speaker*

Personal mantras are affirmation statements that promote the way we want to live our lives. Your mantra should be what you want your life to be. It must begin with "I am"—not "I wish," "I want," "I desire," "I hope," or "I should." Your mantra should also be short and easy to remember.

Here are some tips for creating your own mantra:

1. Jot down three things you'd like to change about yourself or your life. Remember to write them using "I am" statements, such as "I am unattractive, I am overweight, I am unhappy."

2. Beside each item, write down its opposite, such as "I am *hot*, I am *healthy*, I am *happy*." Cross out the negative words that you have replaced with positives.

3. Put these positive words together into a sentence in whatever order inspires you.

Here are some examples of great mantras:

- I am hot, healthy, and happy. Everywhere I go, men are attracted to me.
- I am confident, attractive, and alluring to men.
- I am enchanting, gorgeous, and worthy of an amazing man.
- I am successful, positive, and have curves that drive men crazy.

Repeat these words to yourself at least ten times a day, either aloud or to yourself.

I recommend writing your mantra on Post-It notes or index cards and putting them up on your bathroom mirror, computer monitor, and bedside lamp. You may feel silly saying your mantra at first, but with enough repetition, your mantra will become your reality.

Curvy Contemplation

Write down three things you'd like to change about yourself or your life. Beside each item, write down its opposite.

	Item to Change	Its Opposite
1.	I am	I am
2.	I am	I am
3.	I am	I am

Use your three opposite items to create your new mantras.

1.

2.

3.

CCG STEP #7

Get in a Sexy State of Mind

"Confidence is the ultimate in sexy. There is nothing more attractive, more seductive, than someone who is confident and embraces her life."

~Stella Ellis, author and plus-size model

While you may think that skinny girls with big boobs and tight clothes have cornered the market on sexiness, I'm here to tell you that you're wrong. "Sexy" is an attitude that radiates from within. Size is immaterial; the quality of your "feminine swagger" is paramount.

Think about it. I'm sure you know many skinny girls who aren't sexy. You also probably know several curvy girls who exude sexuality.

Being sexy is a choice—*your* choice. Nobody can wave a magic wand and make you sexy. New clothes can make you look up-to-date. Fresh makeup can give you an entirely new look. Neither of those things, however, will make you sexy. Sex appeal cannot be bought. No matter the effort, it also won't come from sweat or tears. Weight loss, hair extensions, expensive clothes, or a BMW convertible will not make you sexy. Sexiness can only come from within. It must stem from the authentic belief that you are irresistible and appealing. If you don't believe you're a sexy siren, you will not exude sex appeal.

Here are some tips to help you get into a sexy state of mind:

Strut your stuff. If you want to turn heads when you walk into a room, you have to move your body with confidence and grace. Always stand tall and have good posture. Keep your shoulders back and your head up. Swing your hips to show that you know how to work those curves. It also doesn't hurt to push out your chest a little.

Play up your femininity. Men go nuts for feminine women who have an air of confidence. Small tweaks can amp up your sex appeal: heels, red lipstick, a subtle hair toss. You can still be you while adding an emphasis on your natural gifts.

Think sexy thoughts. A great way to feel sexy is to *think* sexy. Imagine yourself as sultry and desirable. Picture yourself with the man of your dreams in romantic situations. If you haven't been on a romantic date lately, you may be out of touch with your sexual imagination. To help bring it back to life, read a steamy book or watch a movie that gets you going.

Smell sexy. Put on some perfume or scented lotion that makes you feel pretty. You can also light a scented candle that will smell good while providing romantic ambiance.

Shake hands like you mean it. Sexy women don't hold back. When meeting someone, always shake his or her hand firmly and hold eye contact. Always smile and repeat the person's name back to them. A simple handshake can say a lot—and you want yours to say that you are confident and self-possessed.

Being sexy helps get you noticed. When someone walks into a room with a tangible vibrancy, people pay attention. Feeling sexy will help you feel more confident and will definitely turn more heads in your direction. Even if you've never considered yourself a sexy person, you can change. You just need to make up your mind that you *are* sexy, and you will be.

Chapter Two

Lights, Camera, Life!

"Stop acting as if life is a rehearsal. Live this
day as if it were your last. The past is over
and gone. The future is not guaranteed."

~Wayne Dyer

Carpe diem! You only have the present, so don't start your day without passion. "Someday" is *today*.

Many curvy girls spend too much time dreaming of the future while not being fully engaged in today. You say, "I will start dating when I lose twenty pounds," but when that day doesn't come, you've lost days, weeks, months, and sometimes even years getting ready to start your life.

Don't waste your life getting ready! Be confident in who you are and how you look *today*.

Whether you like it or not, the body you currently have is your reality. Things might change down the road, but what you have now is what you need to rock.

Fully engage and invest in your life as it is at this moment. Value, appreciate, and celebrate every situation. American poet, Ralph Waldo Emerson wrote, "Write it in your heart that every day is the best day of the year." Try to find the good, even in frustrating situations. When you're stuck in traffic, take the opportunity to turn down the radio and enjoy the peace or call a friend you need to check in with. When your plane is delayed, go browsing through the stores, enjoy a cup of coffee or a specialty drink, get a chair massage (my favorite), or buy a book you've always wanted to read. Or better yet, go to the sports bar and practice your flirting.

Enjoy yourself in every moment, because this is it.

Curvy Contemplation

What is a common frustration in your life? Write down the steps you are going to take to turn that situation around in the future.
Step 1.
Step 2.
Step 3.

Rock What You've Got!

"Choosing to be positive and having a grateful attitude is going to determine how you're going to live your life."
~Joel Osteen

For curvy girls, complaining about your body can become routine. "I hate my fat arms." "My double chin makes me look like a cow in pictures." "My stomach looks like two pigs fighting under a blanket." You get the point.

Many of us forget to be grateful for what we *do* have.

Marie Forleo, a dating expert and entrepreneurial coach, says, "Two thoughts can't occupy the same space at the same time." If you are concentrating on what you're grateful for, you will not have any space for negativity.

"What you focus on expands, and when you focus on the goodness in your life, you create more of it. Opportunities, relationships, even money flowed my way when I learned to be grateful no matter what happened in my life."
~*Oprah Winfrey*

Your body is a remarkable thing, even if you don't think it's perfect.

Writing a gratitude list will help you focus on the positive aspects of your life and your body. Start your gratitude list by jotting down activities your body allows you to enjoy. For example, you can use it to:

- Go shopping
- Watch a movie
- Give someone a hug
- Pet an animal
- Stroll along the beach
- Make love!

Next, make an inventory of every physical aspect of your body that you *like*. For example:

- Pretty eyes
- Nicely shaped nose
- Plump lips
- Shapely derriere
- Big boobs
- Long legs

Next, it's time to take notice of and be thankful for all of your God-given attributes:

- Intelligence
- Thoughtfulness
- Good with money
- Wittiness
- Fun
- Good cook

Last but not least, make a list of the other blessings in your life. For example:

- Your pet
- Your home
- Your car
- Your family
- Your friends
- Your freedom
- Your job

Now that you have your gratitude list, read it over daily. Every time you think of a new blessing, add it to your list. I bet you didn't realize how much you have for which you can truly be grateful! From now on, when you feel a pity party coming on, pull out that list and review it. You can't be grateful and negative at the same time!

Curvy Contemplation

Enjoyable Activities:

1. _____
2. _____
3. _____
4. _____

Physical Aspects:

1. _____
2. _____
3. _____
4. _____

God-Given Attributes:

1. _____
2. _____
3. _____
4. _____

Blessings:

1. _____
2. _____
3. _____
4. _____

Don't Let Your Attitude Give You a Case of Mood Poisoning

"Being a sex symbol has to do with an attitude, not looks. Most men think it's looks; most women know otherwise."

~*Kathleen Turner*

Attitude has a huge impact on how successful you become in life and in dating.

Your thoughts affect your actions and the way your prospective dates respond to you. For example, if you keep saying that you're too fat and not good enough, you will begin to act like you're too fat and not good enough. If you have feelings of inadequacy, you will avoid dating opportunities. You will be subconsciously drawn to guys who treat you like you are not good enough, and you will allow them to take advantage of and mistreat you.

To attract great guys, you must break the cycle of negativity. This involves detoxifying your mind of old, negative words and thoughts and replacing them with new, positive ones.

Say you're getting ready to go to a club with some friends and you start thinking, "Nobody is going to be interested in me, and I'm going to have a terrible time."

Stop. Immediately replace that thought with, "I'm a curvy girl. There are going to be many desirable guys at the club that will be attracted to me. I'm going to have the night of my life."

When you hear those negative thoughts creeping back in, replace them with positive words.

"If you live a life of negativity, you will find yourself seasick during your entire voyage. The negative person is half defeated before even beginning."

~*John Mason*

It is key to approach every outing as an opportunity for a new and wonderful adventure. When you enter a situation thinking it's going to be fun, the potential for it actually *being* fun increases dramatically. If you go through life with a negative attitude, you will probably get back what you are putting out. Guys can sense your energy and will cross the room to stay away from someone that radiates negativity, bitterness, or desperation.

The benefits of practicing these skills will be life changing. Instead of running away from opportunities and adventures, you will embrace them.

If you view yourself positively, you won't allow guys to treat you like less of a person—because you'll know you deserve more. Your radiance will attract more desirable guys. When you engage a positive attitude, your possibilities, experiences, and magnificent adventures become endless.

"If you could kick the person in the pants responsible for most of your trouble, you wouldn't sit for a month."
~Theodore Roosevelt

Random Facts of Kindness

"There is overwhelming evidence that the higher the level of self-esteem, the more likely one will be to treat others with respect, kindness, and generosity."

~Nathaniel Branden, self-esteem psychotherapist

The world is attracted to kindness. The beauty of kindness is that by helping others, you help yourself. Reverend Karl Reiland said, "In about the same degree as you are helpful, you will be happy."

Practice being kind and giving to others. When you give, you are not focusing on yourself—you are focusing on what you have to offer. This will invite more abundance and fulfillment into your life. When you are fulfilled, your energy will attract others.

To get started, try to do something nice for someone every day. To get ideas, check out www.randomactsofkindness.org. If you are really committed to practicing kindness, I recommend doing Cami Walker's "29-Day Giving Challenge." Go to www.29Gifts. org to sign up, download a twenty-nine-day giving calendar, get free gift cards, and more.

"Choose being kind over being right,
and you'll be right every time."

~Richard Carlson, author, psychotherapist, and motivational speaker

You may be thinking, "I'm so busy with work, dating, and everything else, how am I going to fit in giving too?" Or "I'm strapped for cash. How am I going to find the money for all of these gifts of kindness?"

Rest easy, my curvy friends. First and foremost, giving comes from the heart. You can give material things, but the best gifts are simple and free. Here are some examples:
- Say hello to someone you don't know.
- Call a friend who is having a hard time.
- Call or text a friend who you haven't connected with in a while to let them know you are thinking of them.
- Leave a note for a coworker to let them know you appreciate them.
- Bring a flower from your yard for a coworker.
- Pay a compliment to a stranger.
- Let someone cut in front of you while driving, even if you think they don't have the right of way.
- Open a door or hold an elevator for someone.

- Forward your friend an article they would like.
- Offer to babysit for a friend who doesn't get out or needs a date night with her hubby.
- Offer to let someone with fewer items go in front of you in line. (Just make sure they don't have a big stack of coupons!)

If you do have a little extra time and money and want to make a difference, here are some of my favorite ways to give:

- Go to McDonald's or any other fast-food restaurant and buy several gift cards in small amounts. Keep them in your purse, and when you see a person in need, whip one out. It will make their day and make you feel great.
- When going through a tollbooth, pay for the person behind you. I've had someone do this for me, and it really made a difference. It reminded me that there are nice people in the world, and it inspired me to be one of them.
- Leave a good waitress an extra-large tip. Or drop in a few bucks at a counter tip jar.
- Donate a dollar when asked at the grocery store or pet store. A little goes a long way.
- Support your neighborhood kids. When they come to the door selling cookies or wrapping paper, buy some. Stop by and partake in some lemonade at their stand. It'll make their day and encourage their budding entrepreneurship.
- Give care-packs to homeless people. Using a large Ziploc bag, make up a kit that includes things like a toothbrush, toothpaste, soap, deodorant, and shampoo.
- Write a letter to someone who made a difference in your life.
- Cook dinner for your parents. (My mom and dad love this one.)

- Donate blood.
- Bring your coworkers donuts or cupcakes (unless they're on a diet!).

The list goes on, but you get the idea.

After you begin to give and spread kindness, you will notice that the more you give away, the more blessings you will personally experience. You will feel happier, healthier, more connected to people, more excited about life, and most important, more *confident*. How could you not be confident in yourself after spreading kindness?

Give kindness a try. You have nothing to lose and everything to gain (except weight).

Curvy Contemplation

What acts of kindness can you perform this week?

1.
2.
3.
4.
5.
6.
7.

Fake it Til You Make It

"We will act consistently with our view of who we truly are, whether that view is accurate or not."

~Tony Robbins

Okay, you have read all about confidence, but maybe you still don't feel confident.

It's time to "act as if." "Act as if" is popularly known as "fake it til you make it," a common catchphrase generally defined as acting as if you are confident so that as your attitude produces positive results, it generates authentic confidence. Take positive action and act as if you are confident even if you're not!

Researchers at Wake Forest University conducted a study in which they asked several students to act like extroverts for fifteen minutes in a group discussion, even if they didn't feel like it. They found that the more assertive and energetic the students acted, the happier they were.

One of the great secrets to becoming anything you desire is to act as if you have already succeeded. Wayne Dyer says, "Act as if everything you desire is already here. Treat yourself as if you already are what you'd like to become."

For example, if you are aspiring to be a confident, head-turning curvy girl, act as if you already are one. Go through your day playing the role of a confident, pursued dating goddess. You will notice that you start seeing yourself as your character. When you "act as if," you are actually programming your subconscious mind to create the reality you desire.

Here are three quick tips to help you appear confident:

- Stand up straight and walk with purpose.

- Make and hold eye contact. You don't need to stare a guy down, but holding eye contact shows strength.
- Smile. Smiling tells an important story. It says that you're hot, healthy, and happy.

Don't Be a Day-Old Donut

"You cannot perform in a manner inconsistent
with the way you see yourself."
~Zig Ziglar

Day old donuts are not as good or as popular as fresh donuts. They are an inferior product about which people have lower expectations. They are not valued as highly as their fresh counterparts.

Unfortunately, this is how many curvy girls view themselves— like a day-old-donut. This may not be you, but the curvy girls that came before you with the day-old donut mentality have muddied the dating pool. It's a sad fact, but some guys take advantage of curvy girls because they think we're desperate to get a guy and will do anything to keep him.

Don't panic! You must relax and have conviction and faith in your fabulousness.

Some curvy girls become fearful that they will never find a guy who loves them the way that they are. As a result, they abandon their convictions and make irrational, desperate, foolish decisions. A common refrain I've heard from my male sources is that some guys believe that curvy girls are more, shall we say, "orally skilled" because they have to work harder than skinny girls. And guys have been known to take a sexual favor from a curvy girl without reciprocating because they think they don't have to.

While it is convenient to do so, we can't blame guys for this. It's us, the curvy girls, whose lack of confidence led us to believe we have to overcompensate in order to catch and keep a guy. This perception of curvy girls must change, and it is up to us to change it!

Curvy girls must approach dating with even more confidence than skinny girls and hold true to their values and standards. As Stella Ellis, author and plus-size model, said, "If you treat yourself with respect, then men will respect you back no matter what size or shape you are."

Curvy girls should become intimate with a man only when they feel it is the right time, not because they want to keep a guy. Over the years, I've lost several guys because I held to my standards and would not "put out" right away. It seems some guys push for sex or sexual favors by the second date. If you don't give in, they will never call you again. If this is the case, you did yourself a favor. The right guy—the kind of guy you want to date—will not dump you because you didn't put out on the first or second date. Have respect for yourself and hold firm to your values. Trust me: it's better to wake up in the morning knowing you lost a guy for holding out rather than being used and thrown away. When you demand respect for your body, you will exude confidence, and men will respond accordingly.

Remember, you are a fresh, delicious, warm glazed donut (the most popular kind)!

Your Best Publicist Is You

"You are a company of one, so it's your job to write your story, create your reputation, and sell your awesomeness."

~Kat Bacon

Perception is reality, and it is your job to give guys a positive image of you.

Most girls don't understand how important it is to sell themselves (and no, I don't mean hooking on a street corner, of course).

When people encounter someone for the first time, they wonder, "Am I going to buy into this person?" And if they're "buying," that means you must be "selling."

In order to sell yourself, you have to sound amazing, as if a man would be crazy to pass you up. You have to make them think you're no blue-light special, that you are worth a premium price.

Think about it: have you ever seen a sales ad that said negative things? For example: "Dated 5,000-square-foot home for sale. It's really too big and has an awkward floor plan. The outside paint is chipped and dull, and the wall-to-wall carpeting is stained and dirty. There have been several showings, and nobody is interested. May have to resort to an open house and take any offer that walks in the door."

Nobody is going to buy that!

You have to start selling yourself like you are prime real estate: "Gorgeous 5,000-square-foot home for sale. It's the perfect size with a floor plan that will enchant you. It's got great curb appeal, and the carpet is lush, with an extra-thick pad. Competitive offers considered."

The things you "advertise" create the mental image of you that people are going to walk away with.

Similarly, negative comments about yourself sound like this:

YOU SAY	HE HEARS
I'm hideous without my face on.	She's got pockmarks, sunspots, and probably looks like a dude when she's natural.
My hair frizzes like crazy when it's humid.	If I take her to Mexico, she will look like Don King on crack.
My boobs are droopy.	She has *National Geographic* boobs that hang to her navel.
I have stretch marks on my stomach.	She has bright red zipper marks all over.
I used to have one-night stands.	She was a slut who probably has nasty diseases.

If you keep pointing out these things, guys will start to believe you and hear the worst-case scenario. You are in charge of how people perceive you, so remember to be your own public-relations superstar.

Chapter Three

The Male Mystique

"What Women Want: To be loved, to be listened to, to be desired, to be respected, to be needed, to be trusted, and sometimes, just to be held. What Men Want: Tickets for the World Series."

~Dave Barry, Pulitzer Prize—winning author and columnist

Men have long been an enigma to women. From their obsession with sports, eagerness to beat each other silly, and total disdain for the charms of vampire romance, women continue to puzzle over what makes men tick.

But it isn't that complicated. To put it simply: men are looking for something that appeals to them.

You might think you know exactly what appealing looks like to men, but you could be dead wrong. Appealing means completely different things to different guys.

Mike Masters, a relationship expert, writes:

About 10 years ago I met the daughter of a man who owned [a large chocolate company]. . . . I didn't know anything about her beforehand; all I knew was that she was going to join a group of us camping. I remember her getting out of a friend's car and watching the car retrieve about four inches in suspension. She was, to put it bluntly, *huge*, twenty-one and about 300 pounds, but . . . by the end of the trip, I was captivated by her. She was the sweetest, most interesting girl; she was strong, funny, and insanely confident. By the end of the camping trip, I thought she was the most attractive girl there. My mental model of her had these wonderful qualities, these attractive traits pinned all over it. She was truly an amazing girl and my mind radically diminished any physical flaw she might have had. What was important was not what my eyes where seeing but what my mind was perceiving. Attraction is built in the mind and it is in your best interest to build the most attractive you.

Masters is successful, good-looking, and certainly *doesn't* have a fat fetish or low self-esteem. The woman in question won him over with her charm and personality—a perfect example of how curviness does not have to hold you back.

Different guys desire totally different bodies! There are many guys who say they like a slender, athletic body—and they do. But there are also some guys who say that because it's what society expects them to feel. It isn't easy to prefer something outside of accepted ideals. However, many guys actually like and prefer a curvy figure.

Some men love blondes, while others prefer brunettes. Some will only date redheads—yes, I was shot down by one such man because of my blonde hair. Some like a beach-tanned girl, while others prefer alabaster beauties. Some like women as tall as a sequoia while others love girls too short to ride roller coasters. Some are taken with big butts while others are smitten with dainty derrieres.

The good news is that guys don't see you in the overly critical way you see yourself. Guys are turned on by your shape and don't see all of the imperfections that you see. And for God's sake, ladies, don't point them out!

Robert De Niro once said, "According to a new survey, women say they feel more comfortable undressing in front of men than they do undressing in front of women. They say that women are too judgmental, where, of course, men are just grateful."

A recent survey on what physical attributes are most attractive to men[4] revealed the following, in this order:

1. Face (eyes, lips, face shape)
2. Breasts
3. Hair
4. Build
5. Dress

As you can see, build (or body) didn't even crack the top three.

In another recent survey, this one conducted by *Cosmopolitan* magazine, men listed a woman's confidence level, her eyes, her smile, and the way she spoke as highly attractive qualities. The survey went on to reveal that the key element that attracts men to certain women is their "radiance," or overall aura.

The truth is, you are not going to be every guy's cup of tea, just as *you* aren't attracted to every guy you meet. Men are visual, and your curves may be just what they are looking for. The key is to let them see you in your best light and avoid behavior that could turn them off.

The following are fail-safe ways to *not* get a second date.

Ten Traits of One-Date Wonders

1. **Talking about exes**. Guys do not want to hear about your ex-lovers. For all intents and purposes, your current squeeze should be the best-looking, brightest, and most sexually adept man you've *ever* met. Don't talk about John the bodybuilder, Mike the neurosurgeon, or, for the love of God, mention Chris, the man with a member of which horses are jealous. If your new guy asks if you've ever seen *The Hangover*, don't respond with, "Yes, Eric took me to see that movie when we were in Napa for the weekend." No, no, no. Just say, "Yes, I've seen it" or "I saw it with a friend." No further details required. Leave your ex-boyfriends out of your conversations, period!

2. **Flakiness/lateness**. Guys get just as nervous as you when setting up a date, so don't flake on him at the last minute or show disrespect for his time by showing up late. If he has planned a special night for you, it is *not* okay to cancel. Ever. Unless you're in the hospital or dead, go. He's saved that night for you, and now it may be too late for him to make other plans. Stand by your word, no matter what.

    For example, I agreed to go out with Brian because I believed my parents could watch my son for me. When they were unable to and I couldn't find another sitter, I asked him if he wanted to join my family for dinner and then come back to my house to watch a movie. It wasn't what either of us had in mind, but it was the best I could offer. He agreed, and we both had a wonderful time. We were engaged four months later.

3. **Having no opinion**. Guys are attracted to girls who speak their minds. Nobody likes a "yes" person. If you disagree

with something he says or does, say so. If you don't like sushi, say it. If he asks what movie or restaurant you want to go to, *tell him*. Do not say, "Whatever you want is fine." Such a response will make you seem indecisive, at best, or just plain dull. If he asks you what movie you want to see, give him a few choices. Say, "I would like to see either [insert chick flick] or [insert action film]. Do either of those sound good to you?" If he asks you what kind of food you like, answer: "[Blank] and [blank] are my favorites." Never say, "I don't care, you choose." Indifference is worse than bad taste. Guys like girls who know who they are and what they like.

4. **Shallowness/being too materialistic**. Your girlfriends may like your Chanel bag or your expensive jewelry, but talking excessively about such things around your guy sends up a red flag. They'll think either A) "Holy shit, this girl is expensive" or B) "Doesn't she have any interests that aren't related to buying things?" Also, ordering expensive dinners and talking about how you only date guys who drive Mercedes or BMWs is not a turn-on. Guys want to be able to spoil you without it being a requirement.

5. **Man-bashing**. Guys do not appreciate hearing "All guys suck," "All guys cheat," or "All guys are selfish." Maybe you have had those experiences in the past, but that doesn't give you an excuse to take out your prejudices on your new guy. Give your guy the benefit of the doubt and keep your negative male experiences to yourself. If you absolutely *must* bitch about guys, do it with your girlfriends. That's what they're there for. Even this, though, should be avoided if possible. Changing your thoughts about guys from "They

all suck" to "The next guy is going to be wonderful" will benefit you greatly.

6. **Being a chronic taker**. Times have changed. In the days when a woman went from her father's home to her husband's, it was normal for a guy to pay for everything all of the time. But in today's world, women often have more education, better jobs, and higher incomes than their male counterparts. Don't lose out on a guy because you're preoccupied with some dated notion of being "taken care of" financially. After the first date or two, start offering to pay or to chip in. If this doesn't feel right to you, offer to cook for him and rent a movie.

7. **Wearing too much makeup**. Unless they are at the circus, guys do not like clown faces. They want to be able to see your skin and hold you close without getting pancake makeup all over them. Keep your makeup natural looking and not too overdone. Avoid makeup trends pushed by the guy at the MAC counter, and bizarre eye shadow or nail colors. You may have a ton of makeup on—just don't let him know it.

8. **Putting themselves down**. As discussed in Chapter 2, speaking poorly of yourself is detrimental to your dating life and overall image. "One-Date Wonders" are masters of self-denigration. Every quirk quickly becomes a massive flaw. Don't devalue yourself—sell yourself!

9. **Criticizing other women**. Putting down other women just makes you look petty and jealous. Guys like women who are authentically nice and confident in themselves. Putting down other women shows guys you are neither.

10. **Vomiting emotional baggage and family dysfunction**. Don't lay all your emotional crap on him right away. "I've

been hurt before," blah, blah, blah. No matter how compelling, nobody wants to hear about your parents' divorce on the first date. Even if he seems interested in your drama and is a caring guy, any rational, healthy person would be turned off by that. Keep it light and fairly positive until you know him better and have established a solid connection.

Curvy Contemplation

Be honest. Do you have any undesirable dating habits? If so, write them down.

_____

_____

_____

Now commit to exterminating those habits.

Now that you know what *not* to do, here are some ways to make sure that a second date is a sure thing.

Eight Secrets of Dating Goddesses

1. **Confidence**. This is where your CCG training comes into play. A dating goddess knows she must be confident at all times—or at least *act* as if she is. Remember, if *you* think you're the bomb, he will too.

2. **Talking positively**. Dating goddesses know that they have to be their own publicists. Saying positive things about yourself (without boasting) is essential. Find a way to tell your story that's enticing and interesting. Leave out all of the negative stuff until the relationship is more mature.

3. **A sense of humor**. Guys love a woman with a great sense of humor, and Dating Goddesses have this one down. When on a date, try to be relaxed and lighthearted. Remember to laugh and flirt; show your fun side early and often, because you might not get another shot.

4. **Physical affection**. Guys are often intimidated and shy. A light touch on their arm, back, leg, or hand will signal to them that you are open to their advances.

5. **Being a good listener**. Guys love to be heard, and Dating Goddesses know how to listen. Signs of focused listening include eye contact, nodding your head, repeating back to them what they've just said, and following up with related questions.

> "Girls are like Google. They start guessing
> before you end the sentence."
>
> ~Anonymous

6. **Attractiveness**. Dating Goddesses know that attractiveness comes in all shapes and sizes. Being your most attractive self includes being gorgeous on the inside and out. Be curvy, but be your *best* at it.

7. **Honesty**. Guys can see right through game playing, and Dating Goddesses know this. Being authentic and real is essential to finding the right date. If you are dishonest, you may get a first date, but the second date will be a no-go.

8. **Showing kindness**. Guys find kind women appealing. Dating Goddesses know that men are observing them and the way that they treat other people.

Curvy Contemplation

Are you a dating goddess? Could you improve any of your dating goddess traits? If so, write down those that need improvement.

_____

_____

_____

_____

_____

_____

Now commit to adding those improved traits to your dating repertoire.

Chapter Four

Ditch the "Rules" and Get **SASSY**

"If I'd observed all the rules, I'd never have got anywhere."

~Marilyn Monroe

In doing research for this book, I reread the classic dating book *The Rules* by Ellen Fein and Sherrie Schneider. My conclusion? "The rules" are meant for girls without a life, without a career, and without common sense.

Women today are smart, clever, independent, ambitious, goal-oriented, and have a full life even without a man. Guys are turned on by women who are adventurous, career-minded, happy, functional, stable, and have good friends, great hobbies, and many passions.

Instead of playing hard to get and being someone you're not—as *The Rules* suggests—just be SASSY. That stands for Sensible, Amazing, Savvy, Smart, and Yourself.

Sensible. It is important to always employ common sense while dating. *The Rules* was created because so many desperate girls lacked common sense and drove guys away with their neediness and psychotic calling and texting. If you feel you are lacking in common sense, get a friend's opinion while forming your dating plan of action.

Amazing. If you have a life and are incredibly interesting, you will be busier than a one-armed juggler. *The Rules* suggests that you lie and pretend that you are busy even when you're not. I say, actually *be* busy and amazing, and there will be no reason to lie.

Savvy. Clever confidence is key to attracting guys. Show him that you have savoir faire and that he would be lucky to date you.

Smart. Guys are attracted to more than just your body. They are attracted to your mind. Be sure to show him that you can hold your own in a conversation. Communicate to him that you have dreams and aspirations and are capable of reaching them.

Yourself. Always be your authentic self. Don't pretend that you are someone you're not, because there is nothing satisfying about living a lie.

"Dating is a lot about looking good, trying to impress someone, and putting forth your best foot. There is nothing wrong with that, as after you know someone better, you are more comfortable allowing yourself to be seen for who you are. It's another thing, however, to put forward a foot that is not yours."

~Henry Cloud, psychologist

You will always find more success in life and in dating by living your truth and employing SASSY behavior.

Chapter Five

Be Buzz-Worthy

"I'm not single, I'm in a long-term
relationship with adventure and fun."

~Anonymous

When my son was four years old and I found it difficult to get out and meet guys, I decided to try Internet dating, a relatively new concept at the time. I was excited to search for my perfect man online, but I first had to write my profile.

I quickly realized that I was not interesting at all. After getting pregnant at age twenty, I had stopped working on myself and doing things. I was engaged to my son's father for three years and then had another long-term boyfriend for two years. The latter had broken my heart into pieces, but I never knew why.

After some introspection, I realized I was boring, boring, boring. In other words, I had nothing going on. I wasn't buzz-worthy.

The lightbulb went on. It was at that moment I realized I needed to be *interesting*. I needed to be SASSY.

SASSY girls need to be ready to talk about what interests guys.

Current events. Read the newspaper, catch up on editorials online, listen to talk radio, or tune in to the evening news on

TV. You don't have to spend hours getting updated, but a few minutes a day can give you an edge.

Sports. In that same vein, read the sports page to know who has won and who has lost. Remember, you shouldn't feign interest in something you don't like. Keeping up with sports shouldn't be about making you a more convincing liar; rather, this extra bit of current knowledge can give you an "in" when striking up a conversation.

SASSY girls are also open to trying new things.

Discover a place nearby where you have never been. Ask around for a great out-of-the-way town or picnic area. You can ask your Facebook friends to suggest some unique places to go. It is always good to have a few cool places to take your guys to. They will enjoy the experience and appreciate your adventurous side.

Try a new sport. Even if you think you're going to suck, give it a shot.

- **Racquetball.** If you belong to a gym with racquetball courts, try it out. It is a great workout and a lot of fun. The equipment is relatively cheap to buy, and it's a fun activity to do with a girlfriend . . . or maybe a guy, down the road.
- **Bowling.** Get a team together for a summer league. This is usually only a three-month commitment or less, and you can have as few as three people on your team. It's okay if you suck, because you are given a handicap that will compensate for your lack of experience. It's a great place to meet friends and male acquaintances.
- **Softball or volleyball.** Do you have a softball or volleyball team at work? If not, start one. You don't have to be great, and they are a lot of fun. Again, they only last a few months, so if you don't love it, you're not stuck forever.

- **Golf.** If you don't golf, you should. Go online to craigslist and buy yourself a set of used ladies clubs. Then sign up for some quick golf lessons. Meeting a guy at the driving range for some practice makes a great date. It gives you a chance to chat and have fun at the same time.

SASSY girls should consider getting involved in a charity. Giving back is a great way to expand your interests, meet new people, and feel good about yourself. Do you love animals? Try volunteering at your local shelter or SPCA chapter. Want to get involved in local activities? Your local Junior League chapter offers great opportunities for volunteering in the community while networking with other great women.

SASSY girls should consider taking classes. Learn something new about a subject you've always been interested in or just want to try.

- **Cooking.** Guys still like a home-cooked meal, so this is a win-win.
- **Dancing.** Pole dancing is the new rage. Why not give it a try? If that seems like a bit much, try belly dancing. My girlfriend and I had a blast jiggling our curves around!
- **Bartending.** Okay, this may seem way out of the box, but why not learn how to make a good drink? What guy wouldn't be impressed when you order a totally unique drink that you learned at bartending class?
- **Do-it-yourself.** If you own a home, this is a great way to start a low-cost home project.
- **Business.** If you are employed in the business world, there are always classes to take. Excel, PowerPoint, Word, or a good management class are always safe bets.

SASSY girls look for chances to have adventures. What's on your bucket list? Do you have any adventures listed that you've always wanted to try? Now is the time!

- **Zip lining.** This is safer and a lot less stressful than skydiving. I went zip lining through the jungles of Costa Rica, and it was the experience of a lifetime. And yes, I was curvy and the harness still held!
- **White-water rafting.** I've only heard amazing things about this adventure. This one is next on my list.

SASSY girls love to travel. Plan a trip to Europe or Mexico with your girlfriends. Even a short drive to a nearby city can yield a great time trying new restaurants and visiting new sights. Or reconnect with nature by renting a mountain cabin or camping by the beach.

Curvy Contemplation

What five new activities are you going to try?

1.
2.
3.
4.
5.

Chapter Six

Brand Yourself

"You never get a second chance to make a first impression."
~Anonymous

Branding. It's what separates a $15 generic bra from a $45 Body by Victoria brassiere. While all multibillion-dollar corporations understand its power, few people realize that branding can help you, the individual, realize success in the dating market.

While guys might keep a list in mind of attributes they'd like in a partner (a certain body type, a specific hair color, interests that align with their own), a powerful brand could persuade them to try something new.

Think of the last book you bought. What attracted you to it? You probably bought it for the content, but it was the cover that made you pick it up in the first place. Guys operate like consumer shoppers: they stay for the quality, but that initial glance is based upon looks alone. In short, to get someone to stay for your plot, you must first attract them with your cover.

Be yourself, but be your *best* self! There is a lot of competition out there, and appearance is important.

"You are not going to attract someone from across the room with your inner self."

~Janet Blair Page, PhD, author of Get Married This Year

To begin building confidence on the outside, you must start by doing a full body assessment. While you may be doing well on most counts, there are almost certainly one or two areas in which you can make some positive changes.

It's easy to get into a rut and not realize you're stuck in a past decade. Throughout my twenties, I had long hair with thick, uniform bangs. I thought I looked chic and classic—until a coworker's husband mentioned my resemblance to Stevie Nicks. While I have nothing against Ms. Nicks, a woman nearly two decades my senior was *not* my intended style muse.

This simple realization inspired me to grow out my bangs and try a new style for the first time in years. I met my first husband soon after. A coincidence? Perhaps. Then again, I might've missed out on someone with a Fleetwood Mac fetish.

Clothes may make the man, but they can break the woman. Together with the wrong makeup, you might be creating a vision that is anything but beautiful.

I know a certain curvy lady who, though otherwise attractive, was taken with penciling in her eyebrows in a Spock-like fashion and smearing her lips with bright orange gloss. It was distracting to the eye and detracted from her natural beauty.

Someone must have finally told her the truth about her look, because the last time I saw her, her eyebrows looked human and her lips were a natural rose color. (Later in this section, I will discuss how important a friend's honest input can be.)

The following assessment will help you develop your own sense of personal style by determining what clothing and accessories accentuate your best traits.

Hair. I know I said that guys like all types of women, and they do. But the bottom line is that *more* guys are attracted to longer hairstyles, and casting your net as widely as possible will increase your chances of dating success. Long hair is considered feminine (never a bad thing when dating), and guys are naturally attracted to their physical opposite. Guys like hair that they can caress and run their fingers through.

You may be shaking your bobbed head at me right now, but I promise that I'm only trying to help. I'm not saying your short hair isn't stylish, trendy, or cute. I'm simply trying to put the odds in your favor when it comes to turning the heads of potential dates.

Simply put, longer hair is much easier to pull off. This is especially true when concerning curvy girls. Additional length in your hair will help balance out the proportions of your body. Much like dark sunglasses can conceal the effects of a sleepless night, long hair affords maximum flexibility in contouring a round face or concealing a double chin.

If you have short hair now and think you may want to try a longer style, don't be discouraged. You have a few options. If you choose to start growing out your locks, you can take hair and nail supplements (available at your local vitamin store) to accelerate its growth. While you can get hair extensions, this is an expensive (and maintenance-heavy) solution.

But take heart: you don't need to grow your hair down to your waist. Shoulder-length is perfectly lovely, and practical to boot.

With all of that being said, if your stylish short hair makes you feel confident and beautiful, please keep it that way. There are plenty of men who like short hair and will be attracted by your radiant self-assurance.

Makeup. Wearing the right makeup is very important. Guys always say that they like girls who wear little or no makeup, but what they actually mean is that they like makeup that they don't notice. In other words, it's essential to wear the right amount of makeup for your age and complexion but not to let men see it.

Even if you think you could contour and powder a professional makeup artist under the table, I recommend that you call the makeup counter of your choice and schedule an appointment. At the consultation, let the makeup artist know that you are looking for a natural, "non-cakey" look. Ask them for both a day look and a night look. You can be more expressive with the latter, but avoid looking like a Tammy Faye caricature.

Better cosmetics may cost more, but in many cases they're worth it. Try not to skimp on essentials like foundation and eye shadow.

If you're in a rush when getting ready to leave the house, you can skip the other makeup, but apply lipstick no matter what. Lipstick is a great way to add a little glamour without any of the fuss. The right shade can bring color to your face while providing you with a "finished" look.

Clothes. The fashion industry has finally realized that curvy girls want to be fashionable and sexy too. There is now a wide range of sophisticated and elegant designer collections available for curves, so you have no excuse for dressing like your grandma.

The guiding principle is simple: cover up what's not attractive and accentuate what is. For example, if you have large legs, wearing short skirts probably isn't your best bet. If you carry excess weight in your arms, a tank top is not your friend. Please note that I'm *not* suggesting you cover yourself head-to-toe like a nun; rather, you should simply take care to highlight your best attributes.

When I was younger, I was convinced that covering up all of my curves would make me look smaller. My wardrobe consisted of oversized polo shirts from the men's department (hey, they were Ralph Lauren!) and large sweatshirts. While I was going for sporty and fun, in reality I looked sloppy, unfeminine, and *bigger* than I actually was.

Be sure to choose clothes that fit you well—not too big, not too small, not too clingy, and not too revealing.

The first step is to take a body inventory. Select your best physical attributes:

- Hair
- Face
- Neck
- Shoulders
- Back
- Arms
- Bust
- Waist
- Butt
- Thighs
- Knees
- Calves
- Ankles
- Feet
- Wrists
- Hands

I have good hair, an ample bustline, a small waist, and nice feet and toes. I have larger arms, big legs, and, yes, the dreaded cankle. Therefore, I wear long-sleeve shirts in solid colors with flattering necklines that aren't too plunging. When appropriate with the shirt, I will add a wide belt to show off my waist. I wear long, dark-colored pants or jeans that fall below my ankles with open-toed shoes. I always wear my hair down and styled.

My curvy friend, Cassie, is the opposite of me. She has nice arms, a very ample bustline, no waist, but amazing legs and ankles. She looks best wearing dark, short-sleeved blouses with short skirts and sexy shoes.

Fashion is, by nature, trend-driven. However, it's important to pick and choose the trends that will work for you. No matter how cute or "on-trend" something is, if it doesn't flatter your body and make you feel great, don't buy it. Dress for yourself in the way that makes you feel most confident. When guys see how confident and sexy you are, they will take notice.

Curvy Contemplation

What are your best physical features?
What items in your closet do you need to throw away?
What items do you need to add to your wardrobe?

Color. Solid colors are always a safe bet for curvy girls. Worn the wrong way, prints and stripes can add bulk—the last thing you want. People say "black is slimming" because it's true. I am a huge fan of black, especially when I'm trying to take emphasis off of something. Since I have large thighs and legs, black pants and dark jeans are my go-to pieces for toning down the visual impact of that part of my body. If you have large shoulders or arms, the trick can be replicated with a black shirt.

Lingerie. I'm not talking about those elaborate "come-hither" getups that take an hour to put on and five seconds to take off. I'm talking about your everyday bras and undies. Even if nobody sees what you are wearing under your clothes, *you* know. Invest in undergarments that make you feel fabulous. No, I'm not suggesting that you buy uncomfortable thongs or ridiculous underwear that keeps falling down. I'm talking about pretty underwear that is functional yet sexy. It's always best if your undies match your bra. Go through your underwear drawer and toss every piece of underwear that is unattractive, ripped, or stained. Then go out and replace them with attractive pieces. Full-price lingerie from Victoria's Secret or department stores can be expensive, but there are deals to be had at discounters like Ross or T.J.Maxx. You can snag pretty underwear for around $2 to $4, and bras for $8 to $16. You might also learn a thing or two—who knew Delta Burke had a lingerie collection?

Shoes. Guys usually like a woman in a heel that is sexy but comfortable to walk in. If the shoe is pretty, it doesn't need to be any higher than one inch. Don't go over three inches unless you *know* you've got your heel swagger down. A woman that can rock a five-inch pump without looking ridiculous is hard to find.

Handbags. Your handbag is an extension of your life that you use every day, so selecting the appropriate one is essential. Invest in a good-quality leather bag; a handbag will *always* fit, so recouping the expenditure is a snap. When it comes to size, a big bag is a curvy girl's best friend. The size of your bag should be proportionate to your body, and a tiny handbag is not conducive to a favorable comparison. Bags should be carried in the hand or on the shoulder; cross-body bags cut you in half and can result in unfortunate bulges. Totes and larger satchels are always safe bets. When you don't want to carry a lot, select a clutch over a twee shoulder bag or dainty cross-body; not only are they far more chic, they're more flattering due to their lack of a narrow strap. Most important, however, is the following question: do you own a backpack purse? If so, throw it out. Now.

It's okay, I'll wait.

"What do I wear in bed? Why, Chanel No. 5, of course."
~Marilyn Monroe

Perfume. Think he doesn't give a damn about your perfume? Think again. Smell is an important factor in attracting a man. Wearing the right scent can be the difference between the perfect man walking right by you or doing a double take. Every woman should have a signature scent, something that is identifiably *you*. Choose one that matches your personality and speaks to you. What smells good on one person may reek on another. When picking out a signature fragrance, go to a department store and try out a variety of scents (smelling the provided coffee bean "nose cleansers" in between). Spray a couple of your favorites on and walk around the mall for at least an hour. Then take a whiff of the skin where you spayed the perfume. How does it smell? Sometimes a fragrance will not mix well with your chemistry. To help your scent last all day, spray your new signature perfume on your hair or pair it with its matching lotion.

Nails. I can't believe the number of hours and hundreds of dollars I've spent having acrylic nails done. Only later did I find out that guys really could care less about nails. In some cases, long nails might even be a turnoff. Much like bound feet in China, acrylic nails are, by nature, impractical and indicate a lack of activity. When you meet a man for the first time, you probably don't want him to get the impression that you're high-maintenance or impractical. Guys like clean nails, period. They don't care how long or short they are or what color they're painted. They just like them clean and not chipped or dirty. So if you're determined to spend big bucks on your look, blow it on your hair or clothes instead.

Body hair. Your body hair is extremely important. First on the list are your brows. In my days as a Mary Kay sales rep (and no, I never got the pink Cadillac), I was taught that your eyebrows frame your entire face. Without the right eyebrows, your picture is incomplete. Whether or not that's a pile of hooey I'll leave for you to decide, but you at least need to keep them clean. A uni-brow or Kris Kringle–worthy bushes aren't sexy. Next, check out your upper lip. Does it need to be waxed? Mine didn't until recently, when my brow waxer gently suggested adding it to my service. When she brought me a mirror, I was shocked at what I saw: there was a light, short mustache that I'd never noticed! If you're not sure, ask a friend who will tell you the truth.

Shaving your underarms and legs is a no brainer. Now for the area that makes some girls uncomfortable . . . yes, your bikini area. Even as I write this, I'm not sure what advice to give. I was born in 1971 and grew up in an era of hair. A decade after me, many girls think that no hair is the way to go and that having *any* hair down there is gross. I think somewhere in the middle is the right answer. There's a happy medium between prepubescent girl and 1960s porn star. Analyze your individual situation and go from there. At the very least, trim what you have so it looks clean and tidy.

Breath. It goes without saying that bad breath is a huge turnoff to everybody. You wouldn't enjoy talking with or kissing a guy with bad breath. Be sure to take your breath into consideration when you're going guy shopping. Whether you're on a first date or merely hunting for one, stay away from garlic, onions, or anything else with a strong odor. Take along some mints or breath strips just in case. It will give you more confidence when flirting, and your dates (or potential dates) will appreciate it.

Hats. Guys are visual, and they want to see you—all of you. Unless you are going to a baseball game or the Kentucky Derby, don't hide your gorgeousness underneath a hat.

Glasses. Here we go again …. Guys are visual, so don't hide your face behind thick-rimmed glasses—or any at all, if you can help it. If your vision is poor, try contacts. They are downright cheap nowadays. If contacts are not an option for you, wear glasses that are as subtle (read: least distracting) as possible. If you're thinking, "I love my funky, thick-rimmed Prada glasses," that's great, but wear them to your book club or Junior League meeting, where other women will appreciate them—because most guys will not. Unless he's got a thing for librarians.

The date essentials. Every CCG needs at least two amazing date outfits. These outfits do not need to be over-the-top. They just need to make you look and feel great. You don't need to break the bank. Look for fit and contouring. These outfits should include:

- Shoes
- Jewelry
- Jacket (when appropriate)

If you're not sure what looks best on you, take a friend along or take pictures with your phone and send them to your "wardrobe consultants" for their approval.

Get Help!

Before you go out and spend tons of money revamping yourself, I want you to get two opinions, one from a girl and another from a guy. The girl must be somebody who A) has great style and B) is brutally honest. This is not a good time to choose a girl who dresses like Bjork or is a "yes" person who will only tell you what you want to hear.

The guy you choose must be neutral; that is, not someone who may be trying to date you. The husband of a good friend, a coworker, or a brother-in-law are solid choices.

Sit them down and tell them you're updating your look and that you respect their opinions and would like their honest advice. Go down the list and ask them what they think. Be careful to word your questions in such a way that it gives your critics permission to be totally honest. For example, if you have short hair, don't say, "Do you hate my short hair?" There's no right answer to that aside from, "No, it looks wonderful!" Don't back them into a corner—you want the truth. Your friends are not going to want to hurt your feelings. Instead, tell them you are considering growing out your hair and you would like to know if a longer style would suit you and potentially attract more guys.

When asking about makeup, you could say, "I'm considering changing the color of my lipstick. Do you have any suggestions for colors that would look good on me?" If they like what you are already wearing, they will tell you; if not, they'll feel comfortable suggesting a different color.

Here are the areas to discuss:

1. Hair
2. Makeup
3. Clothes
    a. Color
    b. Best looks
    c. Best two date outfits
4. Shoes
5. Perfume
6. Body hair

The Bottom Line

While many women will benefit from implementing the above advice, remember that you should always do what makes *you* feel the most confident and sexy. Since different people have varying beauty ideals, even something that is not traditionally attractive will have its fans.

Curvy Contemplation

Do you need to get a date outfit? If yes, what outfit are you looking for?

_____

_____

_____

Who are you going to ask for help?

Girl:

Guy:

Chapter Seven

Work It Out

"The simple truth is this: when you feel good,
you look good. If you don't feel good, you won't
look good, regardless of how much you weigh."
~Ali Binazir, MD, M.Phil., author of The Tao of Dating

Now that you've got your look down, it's time to address what may be your least favorite subject: your body. Although it is essential to love and accept yourself, curves and all, it is also important to take care of your body.

I'm not going to lecture you on how to eat—lord knows you are already an expert in that area. Some people think curvy women merely need to be "educated" on healthy eating habits. News flash: we get it. Leafy and green equals good; fried and sugar-coated equals bad. The decisions you make are yours alone, and I won't patronize you by repeating what you learned in health class.

Whether you are curvy or skinny, if you're sluggish and in poor health, you will not enjoy your life to the fullest. I want you to wake up every morning with a zest for life and the desire for magnificent adventures.

Instead of focusing your energy on losing weight, focus on increasing your energy and radiance. The solution is simple: exercise and drink water.

Get Movin'

Although weight loss is a desirable by-product of exercise, your main reason for exercising should be your health.

You may already have an exercise regimen—and if so, that's great. Keep doing what you're doing! If not, don't worry, I'm not going to ask you to become a gym rat. What I will suggest instead are minor tweaks to your daily regimen that will provide fantastic dividends to your overall well-being.

We all know that there are many good reasons to lose weight: lowering your cholesterol, reducing high blood pressure, improving your immune system, preventing colon and breast cancer, and reducing the risk of developing heart disease and diabetes. Beyond that, though, a consistent exercise plan is essential to getting more dates than your skinny friends.

"Exercise is done against one's wishes and maintained only because the alternative is worse."
~George A. Sheehan, New York Times
Best-selling sports author

What can regular exercise/activity do for you?

Enhance your self-image. Physical activity will help reduce or maintain your body weight, making you feel better about your appearance and boosting your confidence.

Build and maintain muscle mass. The more muscles you have, the better you'll look and the more calories you'll burn. It's a win-win!

Reduce your anxiety and stress level. Anxiety and stress are major contributors to weight gain. Physical activity stimulates various brain chemicals, that can result in a more relaxed state of mind.

Improve your psychological/emotional well-being. Exercise releases endorphins that boost your feelings of happiness.

Enhance your energy and physical performance. Are you winded by climbing a flight of stairs? Regular physical activity can boost your endurance by delivering oxygen and nutrients to your tissues, helping your heart and lungs work more efficiently. This results in more energy to go about your dating life!

All right, so it's good for you, blah, blah, blah. I'll cut to the chase—how much exercise do you need? The U.S. Department of Health and Human Services recommends at least 150 minutes a week of moderate aerobic activity for most healthy adults.[5] The guidelines suggest that you spread out this exercise during the course of the week. Moderate aerobic exercise includes such activities as walking, swimming, vacuuming, and cleaning the house.

As a general goal, aim for at least thirty minutes of physical activity every day. If you want to lose weight, you may need to exercise more. If you are already doing 150 minutes of exercise a week and your weight loss is stalled, try ramping up your exercise to 200 minutes or more a week or adding in more vigorous aerobic activity.

Even brief bouts of activity offer benefits. For instance, if you can't fit in one thirty-minute walk, try three ten-minute walks instead. The key is making regular physical activity a workable part of your lifestyle.

When you move, you burn calories. The more intense the movement is, the greater the number of calories you burn. If you can't get in an actual workout, get moving by making simple adjustments throughout the day: use the stairs instead of the elevator, take the farthest parking spot rather than the closest, or get up from your desk and walk around the building during your break.

"Exercise to stimulate, not to annihilate. The world wasn't formed in a day, and neither were we. Set small goals and build upon them."

~Lee Haney, famous body builder

Exercise Can Be Fun—Really!

Exercise doesn't have to be awful. If you choose the right activity, it can be a fun way to spend your time. It's a chance to relax, breathe in some fresh air and enjoy the outdoors, socialize with friends, or simply engage in sports and activities that get your juices flowing.

If you hate the treadmill (and really, who doesn't?), consider taking a dance class, hitting the hiking trails, or joining a walking group. Find a physical activity you enjoy and look forward to. If you get bored, try something new. I make my quota by meeting up with a friend at the gym twice a week. We talk (my favorite thing!) while working out, so the time flies. Most days, the only reason I actually make it to the gym is because I know she is waiting for me.

For me, accountability is huge; without it, it's incredibly easy to come up with excuses for why I "shouldn't have to go today." I have another friend, Dana, who enjoys participating in organized 5K runs. We sign up for them together and enjoy spending that time together to just catch up. If you pay and register for a 5K event, you're more likely to show up. If you haven't tried one, I highly recommend them. The events are lively and suitable for runners of all speeds (including mine: slow). You frequently get an event T-shirt as well—concrete, tangible proof that you're sporty!

The bottom line: exercise and physical activity will improve your life. You will feel better, look better, have more fun, and gain some health benefits along the way.

Curvy Contemplation

Do you have an exercise regimen? If not, how are you going to add activity into your daily life?

_____

_____

_____

Get Hooked on H2O.

We all know that water is good for us, so why is it so hard to drink it?

I've made drinking water a daily habit, although I'd still really prefer anything *but* water. Coffee, diet sodas, lemonade light, *anything*. Tricking myself into drinking water works; I'll use anything, from those MIO-brand flavored squirters to placing frozen fruit at the bottom of my glass, spa-style. Sparkling flavored water is the most convenient and my go-to option—just as long as it doesn't really *taste* like water.

So why do I go through the trouble of drinking water if I don't like it? Simple: the benefits far outweigh my personal taste.

The Four Best Reasons for Drinking Water

Weight loss. Water is one of the best tools for weight loss! Yes, ladies, I promise. According to Madelyn Fernstrom, PhD, in an article for *Women's Health*, drinking cold water may increase your metabolic rate as the body works to heat the fluid to your core temperature.

Researchers at the University of Utah discovered that subjects who drank eight to twelve full glasses of water daily had higher metabolic rates than those who drank only four glasses. It's also a great appetite suppressant; often we eat when we think we're hungry, when we're actually just thirsty. Rather than reaching for a snack, you might be able to get your fix by drinking water. Water is also good for cleansing the body by flushing out toxins and waste products.

Energy. If you're thirsty, you're already dehydrated. Inadequate hydration can lead to fatigue, muscle weakness, dizziness, and an overall lack of energy. If you're going to get more dates than your skinny friends, you have to have the energy to do it!

Beautiful skin. Drinking water prevents acne breakouts and keeps your skin moist, glowing, and vibrant. Dehydrated skin looks dull and flaky and can result in clogged pores. Drinking plenty of water will ensure that your body flushes toxins more efficiently, resulting in healthier skin and fewer blemishes. It may take a few weeks of proper hydration to clear up your skin and make it glow, so get started now.

Cure for headaches. Dehydration is a common cause of headaches and can be cured simply by drinking a tall glass of water. If you suffer from chronic headaches, drinking plenty of water could be a solution.

How to Get on the H$_2$0 Bandwagon

The recommended amount of water consumption is eight eight-ounce glasses a day. But here's the good news: the Mayo Clinic reports that other drinks composed mostly of water can contribute to your daily water dose. This includes beverages such as milk, juice, beer, wine, and caffeinated selections (coffee, tea, and soda). However, the aforementioned beverages should not compose a major portion of your daily total. If drinking water is not a regular habit for you, my recommendation is to double your daily intake of water.

Here are some tips for drinking more water that have helped me. If I can do it, you can do it!

Use a tumbler. I bought two plastic travel tumblers at Starbucks. I keep one at home and one at work. I fill one up in the morning at home and the other when I get to the office. To add flavor, I drop in frozen fruit or spritz in some MiO. I personally prefer MiO to Crystal Light because you get the same effect without that aspartame bite.

Carry a bottle. When I'm on the road or out and about, I carry bottled water around with me. This way I can stay hydrated by throwing it in my purse and refilling it at water fountains whenever the need arises.

Look at it as a cost savings. While out at restaurants, pass on the $3 soda or $7 glass of wine and get water instead. It's better for both your wallet and your body.

Curvy Contemplation

Do you need to drink more water? If so, what steps are you going to take to make that happen?

_____

_____

_____

Chapter Eight

Clean Up Your Act, Your Story's Getting Dusty

"My philosophy is that not only are you responsible for your life, but doing the best at this moment puts you at the best place for the next moment."

~Oprah Winfrey

Guys are attracted to girls who have their act together.

They want to be able to feel like a man around you, but they aren't looking to hitch their caboose to a train wreck. Be sure to show your guy that you're put together, and take pride in yourself, your belongings, and your finances.

Your home. If you plan on having a guy over, be sure to tidy up. This means clean your bathroom and de-clutter your rooms. When a man enters your home, he is subconsciously assessing whether he could live in your environment.

About five years ago, I met a wonderful guy at a Cinco de Mayo party. He was fun and sexy, and we had a lot of chemistry. After a few dates, he invited me over to his house to watch a movie. When he opened the door, I was taken aback by the sheer awfulness of what was behind it. I hoped it was a fixer-upper.

It wasn't.

The décor was the worst I'd ever seen. The walls were painted in various loud shades, and he had just redone his bathroom in purple tile (accented with orange walls, naturally). The floors were torn up, and the furniture was dreadful. The house was messy, dirty, and just plain awful. A work in progress is one thing, but the dirt was there to stay. Although he was a great guy, I knew I could never live in his environment. I swiftly moved on, and I know that I made the right call.

My point is this: don't run off a great guy by living in a pigsty.

Your car. The way you keep your car says a lot about you. If your car is filthy, messy, and poorly maintained, your dates will get the impression that you lack pride in your possessions as well as yourself. Be proud of what you've worked for when your date takes a ride in your car.

Your handbag. Do not carry around a bag that bears a closer resemblance to a wastepaper basket than a tote. Dump out your purse and only put the necessities back in. You want to show your dates that you can maintain some semblance of order.

Success is sexy. Guys want a woman who is ambitious, motivated, and engaged in her work. Don't just have a job; have a career that you love. Balance is essential—don't let your career slide while dating. Even if you meet the right guy, who makes you feel alive and spontaneous, putting work on the back burner is never a good idea. If socializing late on work nights or sleeping over makes you late, hungover, or otherwise spaced out at work, don't do it. Compromising the quality of your work will degrade your professional reputation and ultimately hurt your relationship.

Financial fitness. Guys are attracted to smart and savvy girls who are financially independent and secure in handling their own money. Your guy doesn't want to be put in the position of bailing you out; in fact, if he does, you might want to reassess your dependent tendencies. Guys want women who live within their means, are savvy about their finances, and maintain a healthy FICO score. A good financial situation consists of the following:

- Minimal debt (car, mortgage, and school loans only).
- No credit card debt (yes, this is a high bar to clear these days).
- At least three months of savings in the bank.
- Regular contributions to a retirement account(s).
- A FICO score of at least 700.

Many of us have a difficult time reaching these financial goals, especially when we are young and just starting out in our careers. However, it is a goal you should start working toward. Don't let the perfect guy get away because you're a fiscal calamity.

Curvy Contemplation

What areas of your life need some sprucing up?

_____

_____

_____

Unleash Your Curve Appeal

Finding Incredible Dates

"When you dance, your purpose is not to get to a certain place
on the floor. It's to enjoy each step along the way."

~Wayne Dyer

Chapter Nine

It's Not All About You

"I've learned that people will forget what you said,
people will forget what you did, but people
will never forget how you made them feel."
~Maya Angelou, author and poet

Despite their reputation, guys aren't all about looks. If there's one universal truth about the opposite sex, it's this: guys are attracted to how they feel about *themselves* when they're with you.

Stop and think about this. It has little to do with you and *everything* to do with them. A man's favorite subject is himself (shocking, I know), so make him feel like the stud that he wants to be.

While engaged to my son's father, he told me, "I never pictured marrying a heavier girl, but you are in my soul, and I can't shake you. You make me feel good, and I love being with you." What Tom was really saying was that he felt good about himself when he was with me.

So what was special about me? There were dozens of skinny girls chasing Tom who openly offered no-commitment "fun." But I understood something they didn't.

Tom's currency was not about his physical looks. He was actually shy and embarrassed when people swooned over his muscles. He thought people were shallow when they only wanted him for his appearance. Tom felt good about himself when someone made him feel interesting, intelligent, cared for, listened to, and loved for who he was, not how he looked.

I made him feel like a valuable, worthwhile person, somebody deserving of love and admiration. Again, it wasn't about how I looked, it was about how Tom felt about *himself* when he was with me.

So how did I work my magic?

First of all, I was sincere. I appreciate humanity and believe that everyone was made for a reason. I enjoy finding out what makes people tick and what's important to them.

Tom was raised by a strict, domineering father. Criticism was abundant, but praise always seemed to be in short supply. With his mother hundreds of miles away, he was in need of a nurturer—somebody to be in his corner. I became this person and filled this void for him.

How do you do this? It's easy. Here are a few tips to get you started.

Ask him questions! Guys *love* to talk about themselves! I can't stress this enough. And if you are a nervous dater, asking questions is a good way to move the focus from you to him.

Avoid yes or no questions such as "Did you go to work today?" or "Did you enjoy the movie?" Make your questions open-ended and specific to find out what really makes them tick. For example:

- "What was your favorite vacation? Why?"
- "What is your favorite thing about your job?"

- "If it was your last day on earth, what would you do? What would be your last meal?"
- "Where do you want to be in ten years?"

These types of questions will really help you to understand who he is and what is important to him.

Remember his answers! You will need to refer back to them later. Also, great questions lead to other questions. Don't worry about being too personal. People honestly like it when someone is genuinely interested in them.

Be a good listener! Don't ask questions and then tune out. There is no bigger turnoff in the world than someone who asks you a question and then doesn't listen to the answer. Here are some tips to remember when your guy is answering your questions:

- Nod your head.
- Turn your body toward him.
- Use his name when you can.
- Respond with, "What I hear you saying is [insert a short version of what he said]."
- Do not look at your phone or text.
- Do not look around him. Look him straight in the eye like he is the only person in the room.

Give him genuine compliments. Figure out what makes him tick, and compliment him. If being funny is important to your date, tell him that you appreciate his witty sense of humor. If having the coolest car is important to him, let him know what you like about his ride. If being a hard worker is important to him, let him know that his work ethic is a turn-on and that you respect his dedication.

You get the idea. Just remember that if he doesn't care about his hair, don't gush over it—find out what he really does care about, and hit on those points.

Be energetic, positive, and lively. Men will feel better about themselves when they are with you, because joy is infectious. Here's how to show your guy that you're a shining ray of light:

- Smile, smile, smile. This is the best and easiest form of communication.
- Talk about your aspirations and things that you love.
- Act as if you are the most beautiful woman out there (but not in a conceited way!).

Remember, I said it's not about you, but it's definitely not about *anyone* else. Keep the spotlight on your guy, and don't compare him to other guys or bring up stories about people he doesn't know. Remember, to make your guy feel special, you need to make him the focus.

Chapter Ten

Throw Away Your List

"Judgments prevent us from seeing the
good that lies beyond appearances."
~Wayne Dyer

Now that you've figured *yourself* out, it's time to figure out who you want and where to find him.

So—what kind of guy are you looking for? Do you have a list? That battery of nonnegotiable attributes any man you date has to have? I did.

Many years ago, my father encouraged me to write a list of all the qualities I'd like in a man. He assured me that I would be much better off eliminating guys who didn't meet all of my qualifications. My list looked like this:

- Tall
- Stocky
- Attractive
- Strong faith
- Wants a family
- Good sense of humor
- Fun

- Enjoys travel
- Successful
- Likes animals

While I love and respect my father, on this matter he was dead wrong. Had I stuck to my list, I never would have dated (and ultimately married) the most wonderful man in the world.

As it turned out, my husband has only six of the ten qualities on my list. Despite this, my relationship with him is the healthiest one I've ever had. He's the guy I didn't even know that I wanted. Had I held tight to my list, I would've passed him by and made the biggest mistake of my life.

Instead of making a list of what your guy has to be, make a list of what he absolutely *cannot* be. Limit your deal-breakers list to five items. I will give you a little help with No. 6.

Here's my list of deal breakers:

1. A smoker
2. Has no ambition
3. Poorly groomed
4. Has a wandering eye
5. Drinks excessively or takes drugs
6. Separated

If you run across a guy who does not have one of your deal breakers, give him a chance! Trust me on this; you never know who's going to be your "perfect guy."

For example, women often get bent out of shape trying to find a tall guy. Not only does that severely limit your dating pool (less than 15 percent of American males pass the six-foot mark), but you've immediately disqualified a huge number of great guys!

A WORD ABOUT SEPARATED GUYS

As you can see, No. 6 is "Separated." I learned that one the hard way. I guess you can say that I wasn't the sharpest tool in the shed because it took me *five* separated guys to learn my lesson. Three of the five guys went back to their wives; another told me after four months of serious dating that I was a mere distraction until his wife came back. She never did come back, but I didn't wait around to find out. The last one turned out not to be separated at all, as I found out upon receiving a nasty e-mail courtesy of his wife!

There's an exception to every rule, so here's mine: you can date a separated guy if he's already filed for divorce and has been separated for more than a year.

You may be thinking: "Calm down; I'm not looking for a husband, just a date." If that is you, keep in mind that separated guys are generally not in a good place emotionally; their constant ruminations about their wayward wife, kids, house, finances, and any other divorce drama is unlikely to be the basis of a healthy relationship. By the end of this book, I hope you like yourself enough to avoid this minefield.

That used to be me, but guess what? My husband isn't tall and, I think he is the sexiest man alive. Screw high heels—he's worth the sacrifice.

Open your mind. I'm not asking you to settle; I'm simply asking you to give a chance to guys you may otherwise rule out immediately.

"Stop being so damn picky and let go of the mental image of an ideal; talk to more strangers, because it builds confidence and helps you feel more connected; be open to every opportunity, and when you do meet someone you like, keep dating around."

~Rachel Machacek, dating author

Give the Ugly Guys a Chance

I know: when you were a little girl picturing your wedding day, you didn't envision a flawed groom at the altar. But hear me out.

While dating my son's father—a muscular, six-foot-two Adonis—I became used to being with a guy who turned heads. I felt important and somehow special because this vision of perfection had chosen *me*.

After five years of dating, though, this wasn't enough to keep us from drifting apart. Eventually we had nothing in common except for our love for one another and our son. Ultimately, we ended things because he didn't make me happy and I didn't make him happy.

A few months after our breakup, a friend from church wanted to set me up with a single male friend. I had recently seen this guy from afar at a basketball game and wasn't impressed. He had googly eyes, thick glasses, and a strangely shaped, overweight body. After dating "God" for five years, Nate was way beneath my standards. I turned up my nose at the suggestion and steadfastly refused to be set up with him.

Then, one night my girlfriends invited me to an evening out. My parents agreed to babysit and I was eager for a distraction. When my girlfriends picked me up, Nate was in the car. I couldn't believe it. Despite my unambiguous objections, they were not giving up. I begrudgingly got in the car and convinced myself that I was going to have a good time anyway.

Well, by the time we got to the restaurant, I was already falling for him. He was witty, charismatic, and by the end of the night, I thought he was the most gorgeous guy on the planet. After that night, we were inseparable for two years. I have many good memories from that relationship, and I would've missed out on it if it hadn't been for the perseverance of my friends.

As a CCG, you are confident in yourself. You know that you are hot, healthy, and happy and that you don't need a great-looking guy on your arm to feel good about yourself. In short: give the frogs a try. You never know which one might turn out to be your prince!

Give the Out-of-Towners a Try

Many people dismiss long-distance relationships out of hand. I was once one of those people and learned to think otherwise.

When I was online dating, I refused to respond to guys who were out of my area. It just wasn't worth the extra effort. But when it's right, it's right. . . . A worthwhile relationship may be worth a drastic change; my husband moved a thousand miles to be with me.

A divorced friend, Emily, took a chance and responded to a guy who lived an hour away; they're now engaged, and he's relocating to be with her. Both Emily and I would've missed out on wonderful relationships if we'd closed our perimeters.

Give Them a Second Chance

Let's say you went on a date and didn't feel the spark. Unless you were totally turned off and repulsed, give him another shot.

I used to believe exclusively in love at first sight. If it wasn't there from the beginning, it would never exist. Now? I believe in love at first sight and love after a few dates! I know many women who ultimately married a guy they gave a second chance to after a lackluster first date. My childhood friend, Allison, didn't feel a definitive spark for her husband until the *fourth* date.

Remember: a CCG is open to all possibilities, so don't be too quick to ditch a good guy.

Curvy Contemplation

What is on your list of deal breakers?
1.
2.
3.
4.
5.
6. Separated guys

Chapter Eleven

Don't Let That Skinny Chick Take Your Guy

"Action may not always bring happiness; but there is no happiness without action."

~Benjamin Disraeli, British prime minister

Putting yourself out there is scary. It's much safer not to try at all.

You eliminate the risk of disappointment, but you also eliminate the potential for positive change. Sitting at home on a Saturday night curled up under a blanket isn't going to get you the guy of your dreams. While you're watching a *Friends* rerun and ordering a pizza, someone else could be grabbing your perfect guy. Do you want some skinny girl to get your guy because you didn't seize the moment? You might get another chance, but the best properties don't hang around the market for very long.

Famed nineteenth-century author Alfred Crowquill said, "Do not allow idleness to deceive you; for while you give him today, he steals tomorrow from you." If you've taken the initiative to read this book, you clearly have the desire to date. What are you doing to turn your desire into a reality?

If you spend most of your free time at home hoping that a date will materialize from thin air and knock on your door, you are dreaming. Success begins the moment you realize that dating is about beginning. Start where you are, with all that you already have. Embracing your CCG training will help you take the first step.

Don't waste your life preparing to take action. Get out of the house, off your butt, off-line, away from the TV, and get into *life!* Yes, life; that thing people on TV and celebrities in magazines live. You don't need to be rich, thin, or stunning to have a fulfilling, multifaceted life; you just need the desire to live it. Don't look back on your life and regret your complacency. Be curvy, confident, and courageous. Go out and take dates from those skinny girls!

Tom Hopkins, international author and speaker, wrote, "I am not judged by the number of times I fail, but by the number of times I succeed: and the number of times I succeed is in direct proportion to the number of times I fail and keep trying."

Whenever you assert yourself and strive to achieve something, you risk failure. Curvy girls who are never disappointed are those who do nothing and expect nothing.

Listen to me: if you don't risk rejection, you will never get the guy. It's time to put on your big-girl pants and go for the gusto.

Opportunities for guy encounters are everywhere! The best opportunities are often found right under your nose, but you have to be on the lookout for them. In the span of a day, you can see several awesome date opportunities or you can see none. Take off those cynical specs and find your inner rose-tinted shades. You'll soon find dating opportunities everywhere you look.

It's time to take chances, to go outside your comfort zone and put yourself out there–*everywhere*. Be ready, even if you're just heading to the gas station or grocery store. Always look your best, because *any* time is a good time to meet your next date.

A few years ago, my close friend Michelle was single and sick of dating. She called me the day before a Halloween party she planned to attend. The conversation went something like this:

Me: What is your costume?

Michelle: A mime.

Me: As in, a striped-shirt-wearing, white-faced, nonspeaking street performer?

Michelle: Yeah, a mime.

Me: You've got to be kidding me. Seriously?

Michelle: What's wrong with that?

Me: You're still looking for a guy, aren't you?

Michelle: Yeah. . . .

Me: Well, when's the last time you heard a guy say, "Damn, that is one sexy-looking mime!"?

I ultimately convinced her to go with a schoolgirl outfit—and it worked. Michelle met her husband that night. While I can't take *complete* credit for their union, let me ask you this: would she have gotten that first date had she gone as a mime?

While I recommend that you always look your best when leaving the house, there're going to be those moments when you have to leave the house looking . . . natural. Most women think they need to look their very best in order to be asked on a date. Experience would seem to bear this out; not many people get hit on in oversized sweats and no makeup.

This, however, is a reflection of how we feel, not how we look.

Confident people are magnetic; if you think you look great, people are inclined to agree. When you're smiling and having a good time, guys find you more approachable. Nobody wants to be rejected, and a friendly, happy individual seems a safer bet for a "yes" than a gloomy wallflower.

It is your job to be as approachable as possible. Even when you're wearing sweats and your hair is in a ponytail, you need to smile at him and even approach him with a simple question: "Where is the pasta aisle?" or "Do you know what time it is?" Approaching him with a smile may just give him the nerve to talk to you and ask you out.

You may think approaching a guy is too forward, but let me reassure you that most available men love to be approached. You may encounter a man who doesn't appreciate your approach, but that just means he wasn't the right guy for you.

To summarize: make it easy on him!

Talk to Strangers

While you should weed out the guys wearing wedding rings, ankle bracelets, or Speedos at the community pool, you otherwise need to go for it.

Figure out ways to make conversations with intriguing guys who you come across. Do not be shy or intimidated. Guys aren't that observant; they won't know that you're coming on to them. But if they're looking for someone like you, they will definitely take notice.

Here are some conversation starters:

- Guys with dogs: "What kind of dog is that?" "What's his name?" If you also have a dog, you can reply with something about your own pet. This gives you common ground, the building block of any relationship.
- Guys with kids: "How old is your daughter?" You can reply with something like, "My niece is the same age" or "That is a great age."

- Guys at the gas station: Ask for directions to the nearest Starbucks. Maybe he'll want to join you.
- Guys at the bookstore: Ask where you can find the business section.
- Guys in the produce section: "How do you know when a pineapple is ripe?"
- Guys you are standing close to: "You have amazing eyes." "You smell incredible, what are you wearing?" (As long as they're actually wearing cologne.) "You have a gorgeous smile." "I love your shirt. That's a really great color."

Some of you may be thinking that approaching guys is easier said than done. Actually, it really is easy; it just takes practice.

When I was in my dating prime, my girlfriends and I would frequent bars and clubs. When we were uncomfortable approaching guys, we would devise ways to get noticed. One tactic we used was choosing a guy who we fancied and then walking up to him and saying, "My friends bet me a drink I wouldn't kiss you. Can you help me out?" We were never turned down! We came away with many passionate kisses, fun-filled nights, and several ongoing relationships. I was a curvy girl and so were several of my friends, so it wasn't our banging bodies that were attracting these guys. It was our confidence—or our "act-as-if" confidence—that was turning on these guys.

If you have to make up a game with your friends or a challenge in your own mind, do it. The more you approach guys, the easier it will become. Challenge yourself to talk to somebody new every day. You will become a CCG before you know it.

Even the Dull Guy Can Shine

On occasion, you will encounter two or more guys in a group. The assertive, confident one or the funny, outgoing one may not be the one for you. In fact, they may be confident and engaging because they are not interested in you and have nothing to lose.

Instead of getting lost in their colorful personalities, check out the guy in the group who seems shy or can't get a word out. He might be the one who is interested in you. The fear of rejection can cause interested guys to hold themselves back. It's easy to be your best, most authentic self when you aren't looking to impress someone; when you're interested, it can seem impossible to muster a clever sentence. A CCG keeps an open mind because she knows her perfect man could be the quiet one in the corner. When confronted with a group of guys, be sure to get around and make each of them feel special. You might find that you like the quiet one best.

Guys Are Visual—So Get Seen!

Yes, it's true: guys are visual creatures. This can be a sore spot with some curvy girls: "Shouldn't he love what's on the inside, not the outside?" The better question to ask, however, is, "How do I know he isn't interested in my outside?"

As I've said before, guys are attracted to all different kinds of bodies and faces, so getting yourself seen significantly increases the odds that a great guy will be interested. When you are at a bar, restaurant, bookstore, or coffee shop, be sure to sit where you can be seen.

As a curvy girl, I know this can be scary. When you feel fat or unattractive, all you want to do is disappear. Before I became a CCG, I would sit in the darkest corner of the room or, when I met friends at a restaurant, I wouldn't want to eat at the bar due to overexposure. When I learned to love myself and realized there were plenty of men who preferred my curvy figure, I started making it a point to eat at the bar or in a place where guys could take notice.

When you get nervous or start doubting yourself, repeat your mantra over and over in your mind. Remember, if a guy can't see you, he can't admire you.

Flirt Their Socks Off!

Flirting is the subtle and playful way you show guys that you're interested. It can manifest itself in body language, eye contact, tone of voice, and touch.

Flirting is essential for attracting dates. Some are born flirtatious, and others have to learn it. I was born a natural flirt, but anyone can pick it up. Success is dependent upon practice, so don't pass up an opportunity.

Here are some quick Dos and Don'ts:

Flirting Dos

1. The first step in flirting is smiling. It's powerful, easy to do, and sends all of the right messages to the intended guy.

2. A light touch on the arm, back, or hand works great, as does a playful tap or picking lint off of his shirt.

3. Eye contact is essential. Don't overdo it—some people are not comfortable maintaining eye contact for long periods of time. Just use it long enough to let the person know they have your attention.

4. Ask your guy questions and actually listen to his answers. Guys are always flattered when a girl shows genuine interest in their stories, opinions, and preferences.

5. Keep your body language open and engaged while flirting. Don't cross your arms, turn away, lean backward, or look around. Stay relaxed and subtly imitate his body positioning.

6. Laugh and have fun. Show him that you're confident and fun to be around.

7. Compliment him. Make sure these compliments are authentic, personal, and specific.

8. Be aware when a guy is flirting with you. Signals that he is interested include eye contact, turning his body toward you, smiling at you, lifting his eyebrows, singling you out for conversation, standing with his feet pointed at you, complimenting you, standing or sitting close to you, and touching you.

9. Practice your flirting skills at parties, bars, pubs, nightclubs, and informal get-togethers.

Flirting Don'ts

1. Don't flirt with a guy who you aren't interested in. Guys get hurt just like we do, so there is no reason to lead them on.

2. Guys don't play hard to get, so read his signals and move on if he's ignoring or rejecting you. Don't persist when it's your time to exit stage left.

3. Don't flirt at work. It's okay to be friendly, but be sure not to cross the line.

4. Flirting is subtle and playful, not crude or sexual. Be sure not to say inappropriate things or touch in inappropriate ways.

5. Don't take flirting too seriously. Flirt for fun. If you expect to get a date from every guy you flirt with, you are setting yourself up for failure. Play it loose and easy. Remember to have fun with it.

It's a Numbers Game

"Dating is more a process of elimination than of selection."

~Anonymous

My father is a consummate salesman for whom the phrase "selling ice to Eskimos" was invented. He taught me that dating, much like sales, is a numbers game. You aren't going to sell everyone, but you will sell some.

Even if you learn, study, and implement every idea in this book, you still won't "close" everyone. You will, however, close *more*.

For many years, my father used an old sales trick involving beans. He would put some beans in his right pocket and move one bean to the left pocket every time he got a "no."

He knew he'd sell one out of every twenty-five people, so every rejection was nothing but a bean that moved him one closer to a yes.

You must look at rejection like a bean.

You will probably need to meet a number of guys to find the right date. If you feel rejected, think of all the guys you didn't like for one reason or another. Most of those guys are in a relationship or are married. One woman's trash is another's treasure.

Rejection is an integral part of dating and needs to be put in perspective.

Think of all the married people you know. Every person they dated before their spouse was a reject. Your now-happily-married friends were once someone's reject too. It's not that they weren't worthy of love; the other person just wasn't the right one for them.

The next time you are rejected, simply say to yourself: "He is nothing but a bean to me."

"Don't cry for a man who's left you;
the next one may fall for your smile."

~Mae West

Chapter Twelve

Ready, Aim, Fire!

"The urge to connect with others, and to love and be loved, is ageless and universal. No matter what your age, lifestyle, or personality, whether you're seeking a one-night fling, a whirlwind weekend, a summer romance, or a lifetime love, dating is the way to find it!"

~Alison Blackman Dunham, advice columnist

Getting dates is a three-step process.

Step 1: Situate yourself (Ready)
Step 2: Find the guys (Aim)
Step 3: Close the deal (Fire)

READY—
Don't Order a Burger at a Chinese Restaurant!

Do you know someone who is never satisfied with their food? My mother is that person. She orders the most obscure thing on the menu and is shocked when it isn't good.

Bad daters act the same way: they complain about the quality of their dates without realizing that they are looking in the wrong places.

Getting more dates than your skinny friends is simple: go where the guys go. Just like my mother needs to go to a burger joint for her fix, you need to search for a date in places where high-quality men are plentiful.

I know what you're thinking: "That's way too easy." But it truly is that simple. While your girly hobbies and interests might be fun, they aren't going to get you dates. For example, a friend of mine joined a knitting group called Chicks with Sticks. Needless to say, that's not a good place to get a guy!

The first rule of finding dates can be summed up in just two words: *get out!* Getting out serves two purposes: it gives you access to potential dates while also helping you to become more interesting.

For example, a potential date may ask, "What did you do today?" Do you think he will respond more positively to:

A) "I stayed in and watched a *Real Housewives* marathon in my pajamas." Or,
B) "I met some friends for lunch and took a pottery class."?

You can meet guys anywhere as long as you are friendly, charming, and maintain the right attitude. Be a CCG with an open mind and positive attitude every time you leave the house. It's imperative to finding the dates you desire.

AIM—

SASSY Searching

To get more dates than your skinny friends, CCGs need to be *SASSY* searchers (remember, SASSY stands for Sensible, Amazing, Savvy, Smart, and Yourself)—with an emphasis on *Smart* and *Savvy!*

With a little creativity, curvy girls can easily outsmart their competition when procuring those dream dates. If you are willing to be innovative and strike up conversations, you can meet guys in the most unexpected places.

For example, near my house, there's a Sports Clips Hair Salon for men next to a deli and Starbucks. Why not grab a sandwich, sit at a table outside, and check out the guys as they come and go? You need to eat—might as well eat where the scenery is favorable.

"A good place to meet a man is at the dry cleaner. These men usually have jobs and bathe."
~Rita Rudner

Here are some other modern ideas for finding those perfect dates:

Business classes. Have you ever wanted to learn how to write a business plan or use PowerPoint? A lot of business guys take these classes, making them a great place to meet professionals. I met a great guy in my Life Insurance class and only declined his advances because I was already in a relationship.

Bars where speed dating events are held. You don't have to be part of (or pay for) speed dating when you can just sit in the bar connected to the event and wait for it to end. You can be sure that every guy coming out of the event is single and looking. What could be better than that? Simply go online and sign up for speed-dating notifications.

Driving range. Do you golf? You should! My husband is an avid golfer, so I started golfing more when he came into my life. When I spend time at the driving range, I am usually the only girl there amongst dozens of guys. Every time I go golfing, I am amazed by the selection of good-looking guys. They're everywhere:

the pro shop, the café, cruising around in their carts. There are usually no other girls in sight. Why not take advantage of this opportunity?

Hotels where conferences are taking place. Have you always wanted to date a doctor, lawyer, dentist, money manager, or contractor? All of these professional groups have associations and meetings. Find out when and where they are meeting, and go there. A hotel bar is a great place to meet professional guys. Just be sure to look for a ring; a lot of road warriors believe what happens on the road, stays on the road. If you meet one of these, run far away as fast as you can.

Do-It-Yourself classes at Home Depot or Lowe's. The guys who take these classes usually have desirable qualities like handiness, pride in their work, and home ownership. A curvy girl I know found her husband at a Home Depot Do-It-Yourself class. These classes are free and a great way to learn a new skill.

Dog parks. If you have a dog, this is a great place to meet guys who share your love for canine friends. Alternate your schedule; different guys will be there on different days or at different times.

Best Buy or other electronics stores. If you're looking for guys, you won't find them at Lane Bryant or Michaels. Get thee to Best Buy or the Apple Store! When you're at the mall and pass by an Apple Store, *go in!* They also offer free classes. It's a way to meet guys and learn something at the same time.

Sports bars. This is a no-brainer. Guys love sports and beer, so a sports bar is a good place to find a man. I know, I know: "But I don't like sports! I want to go get yogurt and see a movie!" Fun as that may be, your likelihood of meeting Mr. Right doing that is negligible. Try going to a sports bar, especially when there is a big game on. You will be thrilled by the female-to-male ratio.

Festivals and fairs. Everyone is milling around being happy and festive. There are drinks, hot dogs, music, and crafts. There are ample opportunities to make small talk. If you see a guy you fancy eating a Polish sausage, go up to him and ask him if he recommends it. If he's drinking a dark beer, ask him if he likes it. There are hundreds of nonthreatening openers you can use at a festival or fair. Even if you don't meet Mr. Wonderful, you will have a great time. I would be remiss if I didn't give you an important tip, however: Beer festivals are good for finding guys. Renaissance fairs are *not* . . . unless you like your guys odd.

Overeaters Anonymous. I have a good friend who is a member of OA, and she knows a few couples who have met at meetings. For curvy girls that feel OA could help them, this is a *great* place to work on yourself while meeting guys who face similar challenges. If confidence is something you struggle with, an OA meeting is a nonthreatening environment where curvy figures are the norm.

Sporting events. Do you have a professional sports team in your area? If so, go, go, go. And don't just go to sit in your seat and munch on a churro. You have to get up during halftime and check out the crowd. After the game, go to the stadium bar or a sports bar nearby. It will be filled with eligible guys. Married guys don't get out as much, and when they do, they usually have to be home right after the event.

Toastmasters. Now here is a fantastic two-for-one idea. Tons of guys attend Toastmasters, an international public-speaking and leadership club. These guys are usually good catches because they are professional, motivated, and ready to advance in their careers. Not only could you meet a great guy, but the experience of Toastmasters will help to increase your confidence, which is key to your dating success.

A WORD ABOUT GOING IT ALONE

I know it's hard, but try to go man-hunting by yourself from time to time. I promise you won't look lame. Girls who go places alone show confidence which is attractive to guys. Make it a goal to go somewhere by yourself in the next ten days. If the idea of eating dinner by yourself is too daunting, try grabbing a table at Starbucks to enjoy a cup of coffee. When meeting up with your friends for dinner, get there early to enjoy a beverage at the bar while you wait for their arrival.

When man-hunting alone, remember to trust your instincts and respond appropriately to any red flags. Keep your alcoholic beverages to a minimum, never leave your drink unattended, and don't be tempted to go somewhere alone with a guy you just met. If the spark is truly there, he'll wait to take you out on a proper date, which will give you the opportunity to do a proper fact-check on him.

Dating Services

When I was single, I researched several dating services. After learning about their expensive fees and hearing several negative reviews, I came to the conclusion that these services are not worth the money.

For example, let's touch on a popular dating service that guarantees dates with quality matches over your lunch hour. While this company's central concept seems like a good one, I believe it should be renamed It's Just Disappointing.

The process starts when you sit down with a dating consultant and tell them exactly what you are looking for. They tell you they will fix you up on a date at least once a month with a man who fits your desired description.

The feedback I've received from curvy girls who've used this expensive (usually around $1,300) service was overwhelmingly negative. Here are two examples.

Jennifer. Out of twelve matches, only two guys fit her dating profile. One of her dates was a former stripper with a lip piercing; another sported a glass eye. Her worst date, however, was with a hypnotist's assistant who acted so bizarrely that she worried he was trying to hypnotize her.

Rachel. She specifically told her date coordinator she would not date anyone under a certain height. They agreed and signed her up. The first two guys she was set up with were *several* inches shorter than she had requested. She had fun on the dates but felt they were a waste of her time and money. She told the agency she didn't want those dates counted against her tab, but they refused. The service added insult to injury by continuing to set her up with guys who didn't match her profile.

Ultimately, I think these types of dating services fail for one reason: quality guys won't pay an exorbitant amount of money for dates. If you're handsome, witty, and successful, do you really need to pay $100 a pop for a date you could've gotten for free or for a low monthly online service fee? Desirable guys are generally not lacking in options.

Put Your Friends to Work

Don't assume that your friends know that you're actively looking for dates. Even if they do, they may not be aware that you would appreciate their help. Be sure to let all of your friends know that you're on the lookout for a date, and describe what you're looking for. Tell your friends to ask their husbands and boyfriends if they have any eligible friends. Inquire if they have any great, available coworkers, and tell them to keep their eyes peeled for your ideal guy.

FIRE—
I've Found the Guys, Now What?

The hard part is done—you've found the guys. Now you just have to reel them in with your curvy, SASSY self. A CCG knows how to seize the moment—and if she doesn't, she fakes it! Here are some important SASSY tips for getting noticed.

Stay off your phone. No texting, calling, surfing the Internet, playing games, or e-mailing from your mobile while man-hunting. Nobody knows what you're doing on your phone. You might be playing Words with Friends, or your potential guy could think you're texting with someone important. He won't want to interrupt, so you'll miss your opportunity. You must be accessible and easily approachable.

Spend some time alone. If you are in a group or with a friend, find a way to excuse yourself so that you are alone. Many suitors will not approach a girl who is with a friend or in a group. Guys are afraid of rejection, and getting turned down in front of an audience is more than most can stand. Be sure to allow your suitors the opportunity to approach you.

Do not let a good opportunity go to waste. If you see a guy checking you out—giving you eye contact, smiling, and showing positive body language—and you are interested in him, do not let that opportunity go. Good opportunities may not come along that often, so you need to jump on them!

If he is too shy to come to you, figure out an icebreaker that you can approach him with. I don't care if it's the lamest icebreaker on earth, just say something. It can be cheesy, like "You look really familiar. Do I know you from [insert school, association, etc]?"

Your work is done. If he is interested, he will take it from there. If it goes nowhere, what did you lose—two minutes of your time?

Curvy Contemplation

What clever guy-gazing ideas can you come up with?
List a few unintimidating places that you can go alone to pursue your guy.

1.
2.
3.

Observe What He Does, *Not* What He Says

Watch his signals. The last thing you want to do is waste your time flirting with a guy who isn't interested. He may be talking to you, but watch for signs that he is just biding his time until his true object of desire presents itself.

When you see the following, move on promptly:

- His body is turned away from you.
- His arms are crossed in front of him.
- He keeps looking around and doesn't keep eye contact with you.
- He keeps checking his watch or his phone.
- He's yawning. Yikes, he is bored.

Even if the conversation is astounding, do not linger too long—ten minutes—tops and move on. Let him ask for your number. Remember, you are a CCG, and there are many other guys who want to meet you.

Many guys like a challenge, so if he *is* interested, moving away from him might rouse some previously dormant feelings.

Chapter Thirteen

Online Optimization

"Internet dating is the fastest, most efficient way to gather a pool of qualified candidates. It could take you a lifetime to do the investigation that the computer comes up with in seconds."

~Judsen Culbreth, Internet dating author

In Part I, you learned about some great places to find available guys. But as I've said before, it's still a numbers game: the more candidates you're exposed to, the better the chance you have of securing a date and meeting the right guy.

Let's be honest: how many interesting guys do you meet at bars, and how many great parties do you get invited to? Although you can find dates in these traditional hunting grounds, on some nights you might suffer from a lack of quality guys. Online dating is the one venue that puts the odds in your favor.

In the span of a decade, online dating has morphed from last-chance city for desperate singles to a large variety of sites filled with qualified potential mates.

Prior to this, single ladies had to go out to find a suitable date, hoping the guy who approached them had the qualities that they were looking for. But in our brave new world, a single girl can sit in the comfort of her home and look through pages of profiles about guys she never would've been exposed to before. The ability to assess the key qualities of a potential date even before making yourself known is a tremendous resource.

Within minutes, a curvy girl can learn a man's age, height, education level, income range, likes, dislikes, hobbies, marital and family status, interest in having a family, location, religion, smoking and drinking habits, and see a picture of his mug. You can find out more about a guy by reading his profile than you'd find out in two old-fashioned dates.

In the past, a lonely girl might've come to the conclusion that there just weren't any guys who were right for her. Now she can find dozens of perfect guys at the click of a button. Millions of eligible guys are Internet dating, so you don't have to hold out for that magic encounter in the Starbucks line.

Top Ten Tips for SASSY Internet Dating

1. Be precise. When writing an Internet personal ad or filling out an online dating questionnaire, be as specific as possible. Think about who you are, what makes you unique, and your successes and failures. Mentions of moonlight strolls or picnics in the park are meaningless. Specificity is *essential*, and cleverness is a huge bonus.

For example, rather than saying, "I'm a vegetarian who likes cooking and camping," say, "I'm a vegetarian gourmet who loves the outdoors and is looking for someone who isn't afraid of dirt." Include anything that sets you apart and makes you interesting.

2. Be honest. Why waste your time trying to be someone you're not? Deception will only lead to disappointment.

Don't play fast and loose with your age. Your date isn't stupid; he's going to figure out you're lying when you profess your undying love for Duran Duran if your profile says you were born in 1990. Use current pictures that aren't more than a few years old. Make sure any physical description is optimistic but accurate. We all tend to judge ourselves too harshly, so when describing yourself, lean toward a rosier vision. For example, if you feel you are "overweight," select "about average." Give yourself a break. Potential suitors can look at your pictures and come to their own conclusion. Again, being seen is half the battle.

"Online dating is now like eating at Denny's: thanks to Photoshop, in person your order looks nothing like the photo on the menu."

~Anonymous

3. Post a picture or don't bother. Only people who consider themselves unattractive don't post pictures. A CCG knows that she rocks. If someone isn't into her, that's okay. She just shrugs her shoulders and says, "Next!" Since different guys are attracted to different kinds of faces, hair, and body shapes, there are no one-size-fits-all universal norms in the dating world. Here are some tips for choosing your pictures:

- Use fairly recent pictures.
- Don't use a picture of someone else, ever!
- Don't post a picture of you and a friend. It is confusing, and you don't want your suitor to be comparing you to anyone else.
- Don't even think about using a picture of yourself with your arm around a guy.

- You may Photoshop your pictures to remove blemishes or eliminate flyaways; you may not use it to give yourself digital plastic surgery.
- Avoid glamour shots. They are lame and make you look like you're trying too hard. The last impression you want to give is that you need a professional to make you up in order for your photograph to look halfway decent. If you don't have any good shots, have a friend come over and take some.
- Choose a close-up for your profile picture. Your other pictures can be of you doing fun things. It's okay to have a picture of you with your dog or on a camping trip. Just make sure the pictures are flattering. If you're not sure what pictures you look good in, ask a friend.
- Look sexy, not sleazy! Your photo should make you look attractive and alluring, not like you walk the streets at night. Unless you're looking for a one-night stand, you're going to send the wrong message.

A Curvy Girl Photo Tip

Have your photographer hold the camera up high and take your picture from a downward angle. This will make you look slimmer and eliminate a double chin if you have one. Be sure your photographer takes dozens of photos. In the world of digital cameras, there's no reason not to snap fifty shots. You never know what angle, expression, and outfit will look best. The bottom line: give yourself plenty of choices.

4. Only give out your cell number. Until you've seen your online guy in person, only give him your cell phone number. Don't give him your home or business address, and don't give him your home phone number. Only share this information once you are sure that he isn't a creep.

5. Meet at a public location. Remember that your online dream guy is still a stranger. You don't need to be paranoid, but you need to be smart. Make sure someone knows where you are meeting your guy.

6. Meet in person or move on. A guy can be perfect on paper. He can even be captivating on the phone. But nothing can replace an in-person chemistry test. Don't waste weeks of time texting, e-mailing, and engaging in long phone calls. Move the interactions to an in-person meeting or move on.

7. Only juggle what you can handle. It's okay to talk to several online candidates as long as you have the time to properly manage them all. You don't want to turn off the right guy because you didn't have time to respond to his message or take a telephone call. Keep your options open, but do it right.

8. Keep sexual innuendos to a minimum. Be sure to keep your postings and interactions as clean as possible. Although you may have a great sexual sense of humor, you don't want to come across as just a "good-time girl."

9. Review, review, review! Check your grammar, spelling, and punctuation. Ask a friend to proof your online profile before you post it. Aside from technical errors, ask them to make sure your wording makes sense and doesn't send up any red flags. Your phrasing should be universally appealing; you don't want to turn someone off before you can turn them on!

10. Write a killer headline. If your header doesn't grab their attention, they'll never read your page. That would be a tragedy, since you have such a good pitch to make!

First, peruse some competitors' headlines to see what's out there. Checking out what your rivals have come up with will spark your imagination. In your research you'll notice that vague titles are boring, while specific and unique headlines grab your attention (and give a positive impression about their writer).

There are eight deadly sins of headline writing. Avoid the following at all costs:

- **Negative:** *Are There Any Good Guys Out There?*
  Guys will not want to contact a girl who has a bad attitude.
- **Self-denigration:** *I'm Gorgeous on the Inside.*
  This statement says that you are *not* gorgeous on the outside. Remember, you need to be your own publicist.
- **Victim:** *No Liars or Cheaters.*
  Headlines like this tell potential mates that you have a chip on your shoulder and have been a loser in love.
- **Boring:** *Want a Guy with a Great Sense of Humor.*
  I've read more fascinating things on an Advil bottle. Avoid the dull and tedious. Everybody thinks they have a great sense of humor, anyway.
- **Embarrassed:** *I've Never Done This Before!*
  Lead with strength. Humiliation is never attractive.
- **Misspelled:** *Chose me!*
  Even if you're a rocket scientist, a misspelled word can work against the competent and desirable image you're trying to project. Proof, proof, proof!
- **Duh:** *Looking for Mr. Right.*
  Oh, I thought you were looking for Mr. Wrong. Headlines that are too obvious show no creativity or intelligence.
- **Sleazy:** *Looking for a Good Time.*

Be sure not to sound too sexual or "available" in your head-line. You may attract a quantity of guys, but the quality will be very suspect.

Headlines need to be positive, confident, unique, specific, and clever. Here are some catchy headlines:

- Curvy Brunette into Sci-Fi
- Has Passport, Will Travel
- Let's Go Green Together
- Dog Lover Seeks Two-Legged Companion
- Active Gal Seeks Quick-Footed Cohort
- Hitchcock Fan Seeks Mystery Man
- Radiant Girl Wants Guy Who Likes the Heat
- GOP Gal Seeks Red-Blooded Male

Write a Captivating Introduction

Be yourself. You don't want to attract every guy, just the guys who want you for you! If you put on a mask of what you think people would *like* you to be, your dates will never develop into long-term relationships because your façade can only last so long. Just be your wonderful, authentic self.

Be positive about yourself. Stay away from put-downs. Charming quirks are okay; poor self-image isn't.

Weed them out. State what you're *not* looking for in no uncertain terms. For example, if you won't date a guy who rides a motorcycle, say so. Maybe you can't stand tattoos or abide a rabid sports fan. It's okay to admit it. The guys who share your beliefs and interests will be even more interested because of your specificity. Just be sure you're 100 percent adamantly against the attributes you list; you don't want to scare away someone great over an overstated prejudice.

Discuss what energizes you. Whether it's good or bad, talk about it. What are you passionate about? Inversely, what bugs the crap out of you? Again, guys with similar passions and pet peeves will feel bonded to you. Being neutral or malleable is boring and a turnoff.

Be unique and distinguish yourself. What sets you apart from everyone else? Really stop and think about it. Figure out what it is, and write about it. Share your hopes, dreams, and goals for the future. If you plan to travel through Europe, buy a mountain cabin, learn to play the piano, or write a book, say so. Guys will appreciate your lack of complacency.

Be detailed. Instead of saying you "love to travel," say you "love traveling to South America." Instead of saying you "enjoy eating out," say you "enjoy eating authentic Mexican food." And instead of saying you are "addicted to sitcoms," say you are "addicted to the *Big Bang Theory*." When you're specific with your descriptions, it gives your reader the opportunity to really connect with you. It also shows that you're not afraid to share your true self.

The Best Online Dating Sites

There are dozens of Internet dating sites to choose from. Some charge hefty monthly fees, and others are free; some are for hookups, and some are for lasting relationships; some are more general, and some are for a specific niche.

If you're looking for a serious relationship, I would stay away from the free sites. The objective of guys on free sites is often dubious at best. There may be an occasional diamond in the rough, but they are few and far between. Putting money on the line is a good indication that a guy is serious about the dating process.

Most online dating sites have a feature that allows you to check them out before signing up. Many sites will even let you start searching for potential dates. Take a close look at the guys who come up in your search results. Are they the type of guys you're looking for? Test all of the sites, and spend your money where the selection appears best. I'll touch on some of the more popular sites.

Match.com. This is my dating site of choice. Match is recognized as the largest online dating site in the world. It features robust search capabilities that can easily show you your best matches. It is easy to view and communicate with potential dates. There is a reasonable fee for Match, which I feel weeds out the "good-time Charlies."

eHarmony. This is a great site if you are really serious about finding a long-term relationship. eHarmony asks you a series of personality questions and will match you up with compatible guys. Here are the pros of eHarmony:

- The site has a great track record for bringing together couples who eventually get married.
- If you believe in the validity of personality tests and match-making, this is a good site for you.
- First impressions are made by personality and compatibility. Physical images are not brought into play until the connection has been established.
- It is a fairly expensive site, so guys on the site are serious about finding love.

Here are the pitfalls of eHarmony:

- After filling out your personality test, you are assigned a personality profile. If you feel the personality profile does not describe you, there is nothing you can do about it. You aren't allowed to retake the test. eHarmony stands by the fact that their test is infallible—a contentious claim at best.

- Once you are matched with a guy who piques your interest, you are supposed to go through a long set of back-and-forth communications. This can be tedious and annoying.
- You can't browse. You may only view the guys that eHarmony has selected for you.
- eHarmony is more expensive than its competitors.

PAID DATING SITE TIP

*T*ake note of the date your free trial or subscription expires. In most cases, if you don't specifically cancel your subscription, it will be automatically renewed.

Plenty of Fish. This is a fine choice if you're just looking for a good time. It's free, setting a low barrier that causes it to be filled with people of inconsistent quality. A guy seeking a woman for the night goes on Plenty of Fish. I'm not saying it's impossible to find your prince there, but you'll probably have to kiss a lot of frogs first.

Facebook. Facebook has more than 500 million members and is easily the most successful social-networking site on the planet. Love it or hate it, Facebook isn't going anywhere anytime soon. While it isn't considered a traditional dating site, it's a great place to make connections.

My Facebook Success Story

My husband found me on Facebook after twenty years had passed since we last saw each other. Scott was my next-door neighbor growing up and a year ahead of me in high school. His parents moved away shortly after I graduated, and I forgot all about my cute neighbor until a message from him popped up on Facebook. We connected by exchanging some messages, and then he asked for my phone number. I have talked to him every day since! Scott believes he either found me looking up our high school connections or that I was a "friend of a friend." Either way, Facebook is a good place to look for dates because it's easy to tell if someone is single and looking, and having a common bond from childhood or through a friend of a friend can give you an edge.

Curvy Contemplation

Are you Internet dating? If not, what dating site are you going to try?

_____

Do you have a clever headline? If not, practice writing a few:
1.
2.
3.

Part 3

It's Raining Men

First Date and Beyond

"If you do what you've always done, you'll
get what you've always gotten."
~Tony Robbins

Chapter Fourteen

The "Where Have You Been All My Life?" First Date

"Save a boyfriend for a rainy day and
another, in case it doesn't rain."
~*Mae West*

Setting Up the First Date

If you met your date online, trust me when I say keep your first date short! Just because you've "connected" through e-mails and had a few interesting phone calls doesn't mean you will have chemistry in person.

I've made the mistake of planning long dates because I just *knew* that he was amazing and that we were going to be attracted to each other. In one instance, I found an incredibly hot fire chief on Match.com who wanted to meet me. We e-mailed back and forth and had a short but pleasant phone call. Then he asked me over to his house for dinner and a movie.

I have to stop here to explain that this is a classic example of "do as I say, not as I do." I do *not* recommend going to a stranger's house on the first date *ever*. I let my excitement get the best of me and figured that someone who pulls people from burning buildings for a living couldn't be that bad . . . right?

Did I mention he was really hot?

When I arrived at his house, I noticed something odd. The walls were bare, and every room was sparsely furnished. I asked if he'd just moved in, to which he replied, "No, I've lived here for over five years." Was this a red flag? I wasn't sure. But he was definitely as hot as his online pictures, so *of course* I gave him the benefit of the doubt and continued with the date. After about an hour of getting to know him, I realized he was as boring as his house, and I wanted out. Only there was no polite way to end the night when I had already agreed to watch a movie with him.

I stayed for the entire thing and counted down the seconds until I could leave. When it finally ended and I got up to gather my things, he began kissing me. I was caught in a trap of my own design in the house of a stranger whom I didn't like. I awkwardly pushed out of his embrace and told him that I needed to go. He was very sweet and offered me the guest room in case I was too tired to drive. But I didn't want to stay one more minute, let alone an entire night. It wasn't easy getting out of there—but it was my own fault. Had I limited our first date to under an hour, I would've saved myself an additional three hours of misery!

Places to Meet for Online First Dates

I suggest meeting at a coffeehouse like Starbucks or a restaurant bar. A meet-up in a yogurt or ice-cream place can also be a fun first date. If you both have dogs, a rendezvous at the dog park can be a winner. Your dogs can't run forever, so there is a limited time frame.

I don't suggest dinner, but there's nothing wrong with a quick lunch, especially during the workday. Again, you have a plausible excuse for keeping the time frame short.

Save the dinner, movie, picnic, day trip, dancing, or party date until the second outing. By the end of your first date, you'll know if you want to spend more than twenty minutes with the guy.

Setting Up a First Date after Meeting in Person

Let's say that you met your date at a bar, party, or out and about, and you know you would like to spend some time getting to know him. Plan a first date that lasts no more than four hours. This could be dinner and a movie, a picnic, a sporting event, drinks and a game of pool, a round of golf, or an evening at a comedy club.

Because you presumably don't know him that well, I would *not* invite him to your house or go to his. Also, consider how well you really know the guy before you let him pick you up at your house. If you don't know him well, meeting your date at a public location is the safest bet.

First-Date Commandments

Does Your First Impression on Dates Accurately Reflect Who You Really Are?

- Never flake, reschedule, or cancel. Keep your word no matter what.
- Be yourself! Don't try to be who you think your date wants you to be.
- Be sure a friend or family member knows who you are going out with and where you are planning on going.

Studies have shown that it takes approximately *twenty minutes* for singles to decide whether they want to see someone again after the first date.[6] It goes without saying that your primary function isn't to impress the guy; it's to be yourself—your *best* self!

Remember, guys fall in love with the way they feel about themselves when they are with you. Stop and think about that. Reflect back to a time when a guy made you feel alive and amazing. Was it because the guy was hot? Well, maybe a little, but the major factor was that he made you feel beautiful, smart, funny, liked, and, most important, accepted. This is how you want every guy you are interested in to feel. If they feel fantastic about themselves when they're with you, they will want to be around you more.

For example, a lifelong friend of mine got the chance to meet former president Bill Clinton. She said he was warm, connected, and able to make her feel like she was the only person in the room. Connecting with your audience is one of the key traits of a successful politician, and the same holds true in dating. Keep this in mind not only when talking to dates, but to everyone you come into contact with.

Make your guy feel special by:

- Smiling.
- Being sincere and giving compliments.
- Lightly touching him. It shows him you're interested.
- Sharing some of your goals and dreams and asking him about his.
- Asking him questions about himself. Remember, guys love to talk about themselves.
- Sharing some of your lighthearted pet peeves and asking him about his. This can be a fun way to bond. Just be sure not to take it to a negative or bitchy place.
- If you want a second date, be sure he knows you would accept his invitation.

Everyone gets nervous on a first date; uncertainty naturally increases anxiety. You want your interest to be mutual and your advances to be reciprocated.

When you start to feel nervous, remember that you are a CCG, and tell yourself that you are hot, happy, and healthy and any guy would be lucky to have you.

Chapter Fifteen

The Jury's In

"Speak in such a way that others love to listen to you.
Listen in such a way that others love to speak to you."

~Anonymous

Okay, you've had your first date. So what is your gut telling you? Could this be the guy of your dreams? Or does the thought of seeing him again trigger your gag reflex?

What to do next stumps most daters.

If you don't want to see him again, let him off the hook sooner than later. If he was really into you, he may be putting an inordinate amount of time into planning your next date. Put the poor guy out of his misery. Send him a text about thirty minutes to an hour after the date. Tell him you enjoyed meeting him and thank him for the date (if he paid). Give him a sincere compliment and then let him know that you didn't feel enough spark to continue to see him on a romantic level.

Here is a sample text: "Hi Joe, thanks again for lunch. It was great to get to know you. You really had me laughing. After having some time to think, I don't feel there was enough of a spark between us to continue dating. You probably feel the same way. I would love to keep in touch."

As you can see, I left the door open. This is because your date could become a good resource for meeting other guys and experiencing new things. For example, I met a wonderful sheriff on Match.com (if you haven't noticed, I like my public-safety workers). We went on a few dates, but I wasn't feeling the chemistry necessary to move to the next level. I was honest with him, and he was grateful for my candor.

A week later he called to say that he needed another girl for his bowling team and wanted to know if I was interested. I was intrigued and a little intimidated; I hadn't bowled in several years and thought I would suck. But in an effort to say yes to new opportunities, I agreed. I joined the team and, after a few weeks, fell for a fellow teammate (another sheriff!), who I dated for several months. That experience exposed me to the world of bowling and led me to a different team of guys, who've become my close friends.

I gained all that by being honest and open to a friendly relationship with a man I initially rejected. Remember, unless the guy is a total jerk, do not burn the bridge.

If you want to see him again—if you had a great time and felt a connection—it's okay to follow up. Within thirty minutes to an hour after your date, send a simple text saying that you enjoyed meeting him and want to thank him for the date (assuming he paid). End with a nice line.

Here is a sample text: "Hi Joe, I really had a great time getting to know you. Thanks again for the Starbucks. Sweet dreams." This text lets him, know you're thinking about him but you are not going to boil his kid's bunny on the stove.

If he is interested, your text will give him the confidence to ask you out again. If he doesn't respond to your text within a few hours, you should probably write him off. There are always a few exceptions, but for the most part, if the guy is even a little interested, he will respond.

If he does not respond, do not text again, call, e-mail, or drop in on him! If he likes you enough, he will contact you. If he doesn't, consider it a done deal and move on.

"If he's not calling you, it's because you are not on his mind. . . . Remember, men are never too busy to get what they want."
~*Greg Behrendt, author, He's Just Not That into You*

You've had your first date, and now you want more. Here are some tips to keep the calls and requests for more dates coming.

Say yes, yes, yes! Unless there's a good chance you'll lose a limb, go along with whatever your guy suggests. You never know what you might enjoy. One of my best dates was spent on a fishing boat. I don't fish and considered rejecting the offer, but I said yes and had an amazing time. The bottom line: try new things and have an open mind.

Don't play mind games. It's okay to follow some common-sense guidelines, but throw out those ridiculous rules, like you can't ever call a guy.

After mutual interest has been established, guys like a girl who will call them or send a text message. Again, you need to use your common sense—do not text several times a day unless your guy is texting you just as much. Don't call several times a day or even once a day if your actions are not being reciprocated.

Do *not* flake! No matter what. Do what you say without fail, even if you are nervous and sick to your stomach. Your word is all you have. If you say you're going to do something, honor your commitment.

Continue to give sincere compliments. Guys are insecure and need reassurance like anyone else. You want your guy to feel good about himself when he is talking to you—this may be your biggest aphrodisiac.

Date more than one guy at a time. No, this doesn't make you a harlot. When dating just one guy, women have a tendency to over-romanticize his qualities or try to mold him into her ideal man. Bad behavior and red flags are easily overlooked because all of your eggs are in one basket. Women who diversify their eggs will be more particular when choosing the right guy to stick around. Dating multiple guys will lead to confidence, the No. 1 aphrodisiac for guys!

Dynamic Dating Demeanor

1. Do not tell a guy you are dating other guys unless he specifically asks.

2. Don't rub their noses in it. If you are asked out on the same night by two different guys, simply tell one of them that you already have plans with a friend. Saying that a date is a friend is not lying. Hopefully, you are friendly with all of your dates.

3. Don't lie. If he asks if you're dating anyone else, be honest, but don't go into a lot of detail. Until you are in a committed relationship, your life is your business.

4. Be busy. Don't create fictitious activities—again, lying will never get you anywhere—but find things to do to keep you occupied. Guys like competition, and they always want what someone else wants.

5. Don't be too available, but don't be standoffish. Use your best judgment here. Some guys are not good planners, so

they may ask you out the night before—or sometimes, the day of. Is this a deal breaker for you? If not, I would take the date if you are available (though you should already have another date or other plans). Showing that you can be flexible and spontaneous is never a bad thing. I needn't remind you that a phone call at midnight asking you to come over is just a booty call. I know you have too much confidence to fall for that crap by now.

6. Don't stay on the phone with a guy for more than fifteen minutes. Remember, you have a busy life with a lot going on, so don't waste your time on the phone. Save your sterling discussions for your dates.

7. Have an opinion. If he asks you for restaurant suggestions, don't say, "I don't know." Have a few cool restaurants in your arsenal to bring out when asked.

8. Do not eat a salad on the first date if you normally wouldn't. Be yourself! Order what you would normally get if you weren't trying to impress a date. Just be sure not to order anything that could cause bad breath or get stuck in your teeth. I had to give up mushrooms on dates for that exact reason.

"Calling when you say you're going to is the very first brick in the house you are building of love and trust. If he can't lay this one stupid brick down, you ain't never gonna have a house, baby, and it's cold outside."

~*Greg Behrendt*

Chapter Sixteen

Textually Active

"You should never hang on for the person's next text,
ready to fire off a response. This communicates
need, the biggest dating buzz kill."
~Mike Masters, author of Text Appeal

Whether you embrace it or not, texting is here to stay. It has become an essential tool in dating, so you need to get on board and know what to do.

When texting, it is important to be SASSY, not psycho!

If you are old school and want your guy to pick up the phone and call, you need to get over it. Texting is not disrespectful or lazy—it's an efficient and unobtrusive form of communication. Texting is ideal for passing along information, communicating important messages when there isn't time for a call, and for guys who are too intimidated to talk to you "live."

However, because texting is easy and readily available, too many girls tend to turn psycho with their texting. Always be SASSY when texting. Remember, SASSY stands for Sensible, Amazing, Savvy, Smart, and Yourself.

Here are some tips for texting your dates.

1. Only text first when you are thanking someone for a date. Wait at least thirty minutes after your date to send the text.

2. Do not respond right away. This will A) give you some time to think of a clever answer and B) let him know you aren't sitting around waiting for his texts. Remember, guys like girls who are confident and have their own lives.

3. Keep your texts to a minimum. This means don't get into a two-hour text marathon. Use your common sense, but end the texting after ten minutes. Leave him wanting more; guys like a chase, so give him one.

4. Do not engage in sexting until you have been out on a few dates with your guy. If you get carried away with sex talk, he will lump you into the "good-time girl" group instead of the "good enough to meet Mom" category.

5. Make your responses clever. Texting is a good way to show him that you are funny, smart, and savvy. Keep surprising him with your witty retorts.

6. Do *not* blow up his phone. If a guy likes you, he'll be in touch. A simple text to give encouragement is all of the initiating you should do. Do not text him to ask what he is doing or why he hasn't contacted you. If he doesn't initiate contact, he isn't thinking of you.

7. Not responding is responding. When you or your guy don't respond, that is an easy way for both parties to move on.

8. Don't hang around waiting for his response. When you send a text message, put your phone away and go do something else. Many guys aren't as text addicted as women are; you can drive yourself crazy waiting around for him to reply.

9. Do *not* ask a guy out with a text. This will never turn out

the way you want it to. This rule can be bent after you have established your relationship (after about five to seven dates). Just don't do it in the beginning. Let your guy come after wonderful, curvy, amazing you.

10. Absolutely no drunk texting. When you are out having a good time with your friends and enjoying a few cocktails, put away your phone. You don't want to regret scaring off a good guy because you drunk-texted something stupid. Texting anyone when drunk is *never* a good idea.

Remember, in the beginning of your relationship, less is more when it comes to texting!

Chapter Seventeen

It's Your Time

"Eighty percent of success is showing up."

~Woody Allen

Dating can be uncomfortable for almost everyone. No matter how beautiful, thin, intelligent, or rich you are, the prospect of meeting someone new and trying to establish a connection is never easy.

Your dating success does not come from reading my book, but rather applying the skills you learn in real life. You may be thinking: "Easy for her to say; she's married and doesn't have to be out there anymore!" But believe me, I was out there plenty and had to fight through many of the same barriers you do.

If you only take one thing from this book, I hope it's that you recognize that your happiness and fulfillment in both life and dating are directly related to how you feel about yourself and the confidence that you exude to others. Remember, confidence is key to getting more dates than your skinny friends.

You can have everything in life that you want if you just believe in yourself. This will take some action on your part, but I promise it will be well worth your time and energy.

Become a CCG and *never* look back!

Chapter Eighteen

FAQ—Your Dating Questions Answered

"Men don't realize that if we're sleeping
with them on the first date, we're probably not
interested in seeing them again either."
~Chelsea Handler

1. *Is it okay to sleep with a guy on the first date?*
   Absolutely not, unless sex is all you want from the guy in question. If you do, don't expect a follow-up call. When a girl gives it up easily on the first date, the guy is thinking, "This girl has an incredibly low threshold for sex. I won't be taking her home to meet my mom."

2. *How do I know if a guy is into me?*
   Read his body language. If he is making eye contact, smiling, turning his body toward you, and asking you questions, then yes, he is interested.

3. *How do I know if a guy is not into me?*
   Again, read his body language. Is he continually looking around while talking to you, facing away from you, and not asking you questions? Then no, he isn't into you. If he doesn't call or text even after he asked for your digits, he isn't too busy. He's just not into you.

4. *I've texted the guy I'm interested in, and he's not responding. Can I text him again?*

No, no, no. Continuing to text looks needy, and there is nothing a guy hates more than a needy woman. Move on!

5. *Is confidence really that big of a deal?*

Yes! Confidence is a better weapon than supermodel looks. See CCG 101.

6. *What does it mean when he says he has to work late and is really busy?*

He's not that into you. Nobody is *that* busy. And if he *is* actually busy, he will communicate it in a way that makes you feel special and wanted.

7. *Is it okay to order a burger and fries on a date, or will I look like a pig?*

Yes, order the burger and fries. You need to be yourself on a date. A lot of guys feel uncomfortable ordering a big meal when their date is nibbling on a house salad. I say, order away.

8. *Can I ask my date about his previous relationships?*

It's okay to get the vital stats, but don't ask for details. Some guys are stupid enough to tell you too much, and "TMI" (too much information) can be truly haunting. Sometimes it's just better *not* to know.

9. *Should I play hard to get?*

No way. Playing games is childish, and most guys won't play ball. You don't need to play hard to get when you have a life.

10. *Is it okay to make the first move?*

Yes, but be SASSY about it. If you are talking to a guy and need to leave, it's okay to hand him your card and say, "I have to run, but give me a call or text sometime if you want." Just remember that guys do need to feel that they are the chasers, so let them think they are doing that.

11. *Is it okay to chase a guy?*

No. Girls who come on too strong look desperate or, worse, needy. Some guys are on the lookout for these girls because they believe they will do almost anything to get a guy. Guys do not value desperate women and find them less appealing than confident girls. It's important to engage guys without coming on too strongly.

12. *Is it okay to let a guy know you like him?*

Yes, but be subtle about it. You can show interest by smiling, complimenting him, listening, and being responsive.

Afterword

"Developing confidence is hard.
Living life without it is harder."

~Kat Bacon

Shortly after finishing this book, my CCG resolve was tested.

I was on my honeymoon at a resort in Mexico. Like most brides, I had dieted and exercised in the months leading up to my wedding. I wasn't expecting to be thin, but my dress was strapless, so I wanted my arms to look reasonably toned. I also wanted to mitigate any potential for the dreaded double chin to show up in my wedding photos.

The day of my wedding came, and I was feeling confident. I had lost twenty pounds, and I looked good in my dress. My new hubby was getting a hot number, and I knew it.

For the last decade, I had spent most of my beach vacations at a hotel on Maui that catered to families and older couples. With that demographic came plenty of imperfect bodies, so I had zero compunction about laying out in my swimsuit. Sitting on my favorite lounger looking across the pool at the ocean is the best example of a "happy place" that I've found.

Despite this, my new husband and I thought a change of scenery was in order for our honeymoon. Hence, we chose an adults-only resort in Mexico. No kids meant no cries of "Marco Polo" reverberating across the pool, free drinks, and a livelier assortment of restaurants and clubs. The resort was known for catering to honeymooners, which was also a bonus. When we arrived, there was a honeymoon sash on our door, a plate of fresh fruit on the table, and champagne chilling in the refrigerator. We were in heaven. . . .

Or so I thought.

With our honeymoon package, Scott got a free round of golf. He decided to play early in the morning on our first day, which gave me the perfect opportunity to scout out the pool and start in on the trashy novel I'd brought.

After he took off, I rolled out of bed, put on my Miracle Suit and maxi-dress cover-up, and grabbed my sunscreen, book, and sunglasses. I found my ideal layout spot: looking over the pool with a beautiful view of the ocean. Plus there was ample opportunity for "people watching"—score!

It only took a few minutes to realize that this wasn't *quite* the pool scene I was used to. There were no older women or parents with kids. All of the women swimming and walking by looked amazing in their itty-bitty bikinis—not a stitch of cellulite in sight. All of a sudden my perfect day turned sour. These girls were slender gazelles, and I was a grumpy rhino. I immediately started judging myself and questioning why Scott would ever want to marry me when he could have a girl who looked like *that*.

In that instant, I caught myself. I realized I hadn't told myself anything positive that morning. I was on vacation, and my affirmations were on my mirror at home. But they were easy; from memory, I said them over to myself ten times:

- You are beautiful.
- You are caring.
- I love you.

After saying these affirmations, I was already feeling a little better.

I then thought back to the great job I did dieting and exercising before the wedding. I did the best I could do with the genetics and metabolism God gave me. I was proud of myself for that accomplishment.

Then I asked myself what the gifts were that I did have, given that a slow metabolism is rarely considered a "gift." I needed to remember my list of attributes. Let's see: I'm a good mother, a supportive friend, a caring daughter, a hard worker, I have strong values, pretty hair, and I'm funny.

"See, I thought, I'm not so bad."

Next I had to change my vocabulary in my head. I said to myself, "I'm not a grumpy rhino—I am hot, healthy, and happy, and worthy of my amazing man." I had to say this a few times before I really started to change my inner dialogue.

Now it was time to be grateful. I had just had a wonderful destination wedding and married my best friend and the love of my life. My son gave an amazing toast at the reception, and all of my best friends and family traveled from afar to spend the day with me. I was blessed in so many ways that my mind ran away with me. Wow, how lucky was I to have so many wonderful people in my life who loved me!

Just then, my son texted me a picture of my two beloved pooches, Reggie and Chloe. Greetings from home came at the perfect time. The adorable photo warmed my heart and put a huge smile on my face.

Right then, the poolside server dropped off my delicious piña colada. Though the resort was all-inclusive and tips were already included, I decided to toss in a generous gratuity anyway. It made him smile from ear to ear, and it was obvious I made his day.

Now I was really feeling good.

Shoot, I was hot. Very hot. I really wanted to jump into the pool. Ugh, I was starting to feel good, but now the thought of putting my body out there didn't seem too appealing. What if they looked at my cellulite?

I then remembered Eleanor Roosevelt's famous quote: "No one can make you feel inferior without your consent."

Yes, I needed to make up my own mind to be self-assured and amazing. Was I going to let some skinny chicks take away my joy? No way! If I didn't feel confident getting in the pool, then I was going to fake it. So I slipped off my cover-up and walked to the edge of the pool, chanting to myself: "I look good, I look good, I look good."

I slid into the refreshing water, and I felt wonderful. I couldn't believe I had almost let my insecurities about what someone else might think steal away this perfect moment.

By the time I got out, I didn't care who saw me. I was back in charge of my attitude and confidence. When Scott arrived back from golf, I was in a great state of mind. I knew I was the right woman for him, and he didn't even seem to notice the other girls who had caused me so much angst earlier. I had been faced with my feelings of insecurity and had to remind myself of my own advice. It took a few mantras and some self-reflection, but it worked.

I know I will be challenged in the future, but I am certain I can work through it. I am winning my own self-confidence battle, and so can you.

Congratulations—You Are Now a CCG!

You must continue to take action and to practice being a CCG if you want to get more dates than your skinny friends. Thinking about it is not enough. Continue to work on your Curvy Contemplations; you can download a Curvy Contemplations Action Guide that includes all of the exercises in this book at www. getmoredatesthanyourskinnyfriends.com or at www.curvygirl-lifestylecoach.com.

Remember, the world needs you just the way you are, curves and all! Continue to strive to be the best *you* that you can be.

Sources

1. "Overweight and Obesity in the U.S.," FRAC: Food Research and Action Center, 2010, http://frac.org/ initiatives/hunger-and-obesity/obesity-in-the-us/.

2. "Why the Modeling Industry Should Conform to the Average Size Woman," HubPages, September 24, 2009, http://poeticlady87.hubpages.com/hub/Why-the-Modeling-Industry-Should-Conform-to-the-Average-Size-Woman.

3. News Staff, "It's A Fat World After All - 40 Percent Of Men Worldwide Are Overweight," Science 2.0, October 22, 2007, http://www.science20.com/news_account/ its_a_fat_world_after_all_40_percent_of_men_world-wide_are_overweight.

4. "Attractive Women Survey," HubPages, May 14, 2012, http://ayahajime.hubpages.com/hub/ Attractive-Women-Attractive-Woman-Survey.

5. "Stress management," Mayo Clinic, July 21, 2012, http://www.mayoclinic.com/health/exercise-and-stress/ SR00036/NSECTIONGROUP=2.

6. Anna Breslaw, "Guess How Long It Takes For a Dude To Decide He Wants a Second Date with You?" *Glamour*, March 8, 2012, http://www.glamour.com/sex-love-life/blogs/smitten/2012/03/guess-how-long-it-takes-for-a.html.

About the Author

Kat Bacon, founder of Curvy Girl Lifestyle Coach and creator of the Seven-Step CCG Action Plan, is a dating expert and lifelong curvy girl. She believes that confidence is the building block upon which all successes in life must be built.

Bacon is passionate about helping other curvy girls succeed in their dating and personal lives. Her curvy-girl dating advice is encouraging, personal, and to the point. Bacon is living proof that dating success depends upon what you do with yourself, not on what you already have.

Bacon has been an executive in the financial services-industry since 1994. Her career has helped her to hone her marketing expertise and develop relationship skills that have carried her into her second career as a curvy-girl lifestyle coach.

Bacon resides in Folsom, California, with her husband and two dogs.